IRELAND

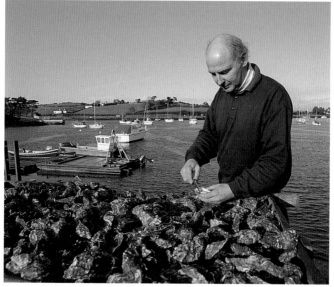

BY
ERIC AND RUTH BAILEY

AA

Produced by AA Publishing

Written by Eric and Ruth Bailey

Original photography by Christopher Hill, Steffan Hill and Michael Short

Edited, designed and produced by AA Publishing. Maps © The Automobile Association 1994, 1996

Distributed in the United Kingdom by AA Publishing, Norfolk House, Priestley Road, Basingstoke, Hampshire RG24 9NY.

© The Automobile Association 1994, 1996
First published 1994; Revised second edition 1996

A CIP catalogue record for this book is available from the British Library

ISBN 0 7495 1348 9

Published by AA Publishing (a trading name of Automobile Association Developments Limited, whose registered office is Norfolk House, Priestley Road, Basingstoke, Hampshire RG24 9NY. Registered number 1878835) and the Thomas Cook Group Ltd.

Colour separation: BTB Colour Reproduction, Whitchurch, Hampshire. Printed by Edicoes ASA, Oporto, Portugal.

Front cover: *Dan Foley's Pub, Anascaul, County Kerry*; Back cover: *Connemara lake; Inishmore island graveyard*; Title page: *oysters at Strangford;* Above: *Blake's Bar, Enniskillen* **Cover picture credits** AA Photo Library (S Hill): Back cover bottom; Pictures Colour Library Ltd: Front cover; Spectrum Colour Library: Spine, Back cover top

Contents

About this Book

BACKGROUND

FIRST STEPS

WHAT TO SEE

GETTING AWAY FROM IT ALL

DIRECTORY

This book is divided into five sections, identified by the above colour coding.

TELEPHONE NUMBERS
If you have difficulty in reaching any of the telephone numbers in this book, dial 1190 (Republic of Ireland) or 192 (N. Ireland) for assistance.

Background gives an introduction to the country – its history, geography, politics, culture.

First Steps offers practical advice on arriving and getting around.

What to See is an alphabetical listing of places to visit, divided into four regions, interspersed with walks and tours.

Getting Away From it All highlights places off the beaten track where it's possible to relax and enjoy peace and quiet.

Finally, the **Directory** provides practical information – from shopping and entertainment to children and sport, including a section on business matters. Special highly illustrated features on specific aspects of the country appear throughout the book.

Ireland's landscape of broad plains and gently rolling green hills

BACKGROUND

'I am beginning to find out now,
that a man ought to be
forty years in the country instead
of three months, and then he
wouldn't be able to write about it.
I wonder who does understand the
place?'

WILLIAM THACKERAY,
Letter to Mrs Carmichael-Smyth (1842)

Introduction

*I*reland means different things to different people, but some things are common to everyone. Everybody remarks on the natural and sincere warmth of the welcome they get from the Irish people. Nobody can fail to appreciate the landscapes and seascapes – sometimes spectacular and wild, sometimes beautiful, other times merely pretty.

The early Christian and prehistoric megaliths, dolmens, round towers and ruins are awe-inspiring, often mysterious. Coming across them casually, sometimes unexpectedly, both in the town and the countryside evokes a profound sense of antiquity.

Another thing that cannot go unnoticed in Ireland is that the elements rarely keep still for long. You could stand in one spot watching the changing scene. Blue sky, contrasting sunlight and shadow. Two minutes later, banking clouds, sun in and out. After that, grey streaks the sky – reach for your umbrella. The grey thickens into rolling swaths, almost navy blue, then out comes the sun, with a rainbow, or two, for company. The landscape responds to the fickle weather, bright or hazy, picked out in distant detail, suddenly brooding.

Dublin is a flirtatious city, captivating its visitors. Belfast has dignity. Wexford, Waterford, Cork – all have their own distinctive character. And everywhere the seafood is sublime. Most visitors appreciate the social life, which takes place to a large extent in the many

ATLANTIC OCEAN | SCOTLAND | North Sea

NORTHERN IRELAND ■Belfast | UNITED KINGDOM

REPUBLIC OF IRELAND ■Dublin | ENGLAND | WALES

■London

FRANCE

Rolling moorlands in the Wicklow Mountains

IRELAND – COUNTIES AND REGIONS

Dublin & Leinster
Munster
Connacht
Ulster

Donegal
Lifford
Londonderry
Antrim

NORTHERN
IRELAND ■Belfast

Tyrone

Sligo
Fermanagh
Armagh
Down

Leitrim
Monaghan
Monaghan

Mayo
Sligo
Carrick-on-Shannon
Cavan
Dundalk

Castlebar
Roscommon
Cavan
Louth

Roscommon
Longford
Longford
Navan

Mullingar
Meath

Galway
West Meath
Dublin
■Dublin

Galway
Tullamore
Naas

Offaly
Kildare

REPUBLIC OF
IRELAND
Portlaoise
Wicklow
Wicklow

Clare
Laois

Ennis
Carlow

Tipperary
Kilkenny
Carlow

Limerick
Kilkenny

Limerick
Wexford

Clonmel

Tralee
Wexford

Kerry
Cork
Waterford
Waterford

Cork

0   50   100 km
0   50 miles

friendly pubs and bars.

But Ireland is essentially rural. There is rarely too much traffic for the roads and if you come to a hold-up it will probably be cows crossing for milking, or sheep moving to fresh pastures.

History

About 6000BC

Mesolithic settlers cross to northeast Ireland from the west coast of Scotland.

About 3000BC

Neolithic immigrants introduce agriculture, weaving and pottery and begin building huge megaliths.

About 600BC

Celts arrive from Britain and France; Ireland is divided into provinces.

About AD350

Christianity arrives in Ireland.

432

St Patrick arrives.

795

Full-scale invasion by the Vikings.

1014

High King BrianBorú defeats the Vikings at Clontarf, but his murder prevents unification of Ireland.

1169

The Anglo-Norman 'Strongbow' helps Dermot MacMurrough, deposed King of Leinster, to regain his throne.

1172

England's Henry II is made overlord of Ireland, opening the way for the establishment of Anglo-Norman estates.

1366

The Statutes of Kilkenny forbid inter-marriage with the Irish, who are also banned from cities, and makes the adoption of Irish names, customs and language illegal.

1534–40

Lord Offaly stages an insurrection after Henry VIII breaks with the Catholic Church; Offaly and five brothers are executed when the insurrection fails.

1541

Henry VIII forces Irish chiefs to surrender their lands.

1558–1603

Elizabeth I tightens English hold on Ireland and launches the 'Plantation' policy, establishing English and Scottish settlers on land seized from the Irish.

1595–1603

Hugh O'Neill, Earl of Tyrone, leads a rebellion, but has to surrender.

1607

O'Neill leads other chiefs in the 'Flight of the Earls' to Europe.

1641

Belief that Charles I of England is a Catholic sympathiser provokes rebellion in Ulster and Civil War in England.

1649

Oliver Cromwell invades Ireland after defeating and executing Charles I; thousands of Irish are massacred.

1653

Under the Act of Settlement, Cromwell's opponents have their lands seized.

1689–90

King James II of England flees to Ireland after being deposed. He is defeated by William III at the Battle of the Boyne.

1704

The first of a number of laws to be known as the Penal Code restrict Catholic land-owning and subsequently ban Catholics from voting, attending schools and military service.

1775

The American War of Independence promotes unrest in Ireland.

1782

Grattan's Parliament – named after Henry Grattan – persuades the British government that the time has come for Catholic emancipation and Irish independence, but nothing comes of it.

1798
United Irishmen, led by Wolfe Tone, stage an uprising which is crushed.

1800
Ireland becomes part of Britain under the Act of Union.

1829
The Catholic Emancipation Act is passed after Daniel O'Connell, 'The Liberator', gains a seat at Westminster.

1845–8
Ireland's population is reduced by some 2 million following death due to potato crop failures, and emigration.

1881
Charles Stewart Parnell, leader of the Home Rule Party, encourages the Irish to defy difficult landlords.

1905–8
The Sinn Fein party is founded after the defeat of two Home Rule bills.

1914
Implementation of Home Rule is postponed because of the outbreak of war.

1916
The Irish Republican Brotherhood stages insurrection in Dublin – the Easter Rising; when the rebellion fails 16 of its leaders are executed.

1920–1
Fighting breaks out between Britain and Ireland; the Anglo-Irish Treaty creates the Irish Free State and allows six counties to remain part of Britain.

1922
The Treaty is rejected by Republicans and civil war breaks out. The war ends when Eamonn De Valera, founder of the Fianna Fáil party, is arrested.

1932
De Valera is elected President of the Irish Free State.

1949
The Republic of Ireland is created.

1969
There is rioting between Catholics and Protestants during the annual Apprentice Boys' March in Londonderry. British troops are called in to keep the peace. The Provisional IRA launches an intensive campaign of violence.

1972
Thirteen unarmed demonstrators are shot by British troops on 30 January – 'Bloody Sunday'. Stormont is suspended and Westminster imposes direct rule. Severe emergency laws are enforced as acts of terrorism by both sides continue.

1986
Under the Anglo-Irish Agreement, the Republic gains a stronger say in Northern affairs.

1994
IRA and Loyalist paramilitary announce ceasefire nine months after signing of Downing Street Declaration by Britain and Ireland.

Parnell, 19th-century nationalist leader

EARLY HISTORY

Prehistory lives on in Ireland today. A prolific heritage of field monuments – stone circles, dolmens, passage graves and Celtic forts – dating from thousands of years BC, provides a source of wonder and meditation. They can be found almost everywhere. Many are signposted, and the visitor casually encounters unspoiled ancient monuments which most countries would greedily exploit.

Visiting some of them may involve a walk through muddy farmland. Such is the case of the pagan Janus figure, a squat Celtic idol facing both ways in a tiny Fermanagh graveyard on Boa Island. Others, like the great Newgrange tumulus in Co Meath, are easily accessible and present a sophisticated approach to tourism.

Ancient religious monuments dedicated to the old gods, pagan fertility symbols, final resting places, primitive calendars – the purpose for which these monuments were constructed is often a matter of academic debate.

One of the country's most interesting surviving mounds is at the Hill of Tara, in Co Meath. Originally including a hill fort and several ring forts, it was the residence of the High Kings of Ireland over many centuries.

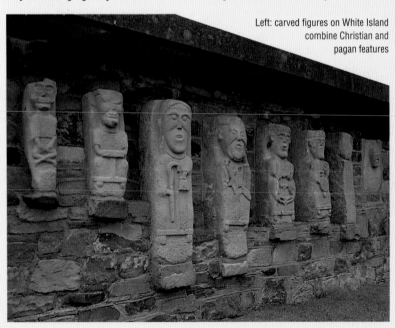

Left: carved figures on White Island combine Christian and pagan features

Left: the two-faced, stone-carved Janus figure in Caldragh churchyard, Boa Island, exerts a brooding fascination

Above: Kilnaraune pillar stone, engraved with symbolic scenes
Left: entrance to Bronze Age Newgrange tomb

Visitors can see the entrance to a passage grave where finds included the cremated remains of 40 people, and various utensils, which have been carbon-dated at 2000BC. Also found was the skeleton of a teenage boy wearing a necklace of amber, jet and bronze. His was the only body not cremated.

Celtic crosses, or high crosses, usually very decorative, stand proudly in churchyards throughout Ireland, dating from the early 12th century onwards, some depicting scenes from the scriptures.

Geography

*I*reland lies on the continental shelf to the west of the European mainland. On the east it is separated from Britain by the Irish Sea. To the northeast, the North Channel brings Scotland to within 21km of the Antrim coast. To the west lies the vastness of the Atlantic Ocean, while to the south St George's Channel separates Ireland from France.

Two great mountain ranges converge in Ireland. The older Caledonian system extending from Scandinavia and Scotland to the north and west of Ireland, gives rise to the rugged terrain of Counties Donegal, Galway and Mayo. The younger Armorican system extends from central Europe through Brittany to southwest Ireland, culminating in 1,041m-high Carrauntoohill, the country's highest mountain, in Macgillycuddy's Reeks. Killarney's celebrated 'lakes and fells' are on the eastern slopes of the Reeks.

A narrow belt of lowland crosses the country from the Carlingford Peninsula and the Wicklow Mountains in the east to the Atlantic Ocean in the west, along the Shannon Estuary, Galway Bay, Clew Bay and Donegal Bay. In Co Clare, the lowland rises westward, terminating at the magnificent Cliffs of Moher.

The stately 340km-long River Shannon is the largest of Ireland's rivers. Rising in Co Leitrim, it opens up into a series of attractive lakes before reaching its broad, indented estuary between Counties Clare and Limerick.

The main eastward-flowing rivers are the Lagan, which runs to the sea at Belfast; the Liffey, with Dublin at its mouth; and the Slaney, which meets the sea at Wexford. In Ulster, the River Erne flows north, opening into Upper and Lower Lough Erne before entering Donegal Bay.

Ireland's climate is legendary, and there is some truth in the joke that observes: 'When you can see the mountain it means it is going to rain; when you cannot see it, it is raining.' In reality, though, the climate is mild and without extremes, due largely to the Gulf Stream, whose relatively warm waters wash Ireland's shores.

The heaviest rainfall is in Donegal,

The Giant's Causeway – 40,000 hexagonal basalt columns formed by volcanic rock as it cooled, 60 million years ago

Kerry and Mayo, where it may exceed 3,000mm. Eastern Ireland is much drier, with Dublin averaging only 785mm a year.

Two bonuses, however, arise from Ireland's variable weather: the constantly changing light and verdant vegetation. Though limited, the flora has many interesting features. The lanes of Cork and Kerry, for example, are noted for their profuse fuchsia hedgerows, while an Arctic-Alpine flora thrives in the Burren in Co Clare.

Among Ireland's 27 mammal species are red deer, pine martens, badgers, hares, otters and stoats. The only reptile is the common lizard. Rivers and lakes are rich in salmon, trout and char, as well as coarse fish. Around 125 species of wild birds breed in the island and more than 250 visiting species have been recorded.

The meandering valley of Glenmacnass in the Wicklow Mountains

THOMAS COOK'S IRELAND

After organising an excursion to Liverpool in 1846, Thomas Cook set off for Ireland in 1853. Following some difficulty in obtaining facilities from railway managers, a series of tours was set up by John Mason Cook, Thomas Cook's son.

An office was established in Dublin in 1874, and by the end of the century a special brochure advertised tours to every part of Ireland. At that time there were offices in Dublin, Belfast, Queenstown and Cork.

During World War II the Belfast office remained open and was heavily involved in the movement of Allied troops.

Politics

*F*or outsiders, one issue dominates all Irish politics – 'the Troubles'. While it is true that serious political unrest continues, the majority of people – north and south of the border – lead peaceful lives and are able to focus on normal domestic political issues.

However, even though the easy-going Irish can – and do – talk about any subject under the sun, politics, while not taboo, is a topic best avoided by visitors. This advice, which also embraces religion, is frequently meted out to people travelling anywhere in the world, but is particularly applied to Ireland, because even the most reasonable character can get hot under the collar when a stranger talks Irish politics in a less-than-knowledgeable way.

Politicians from the Republic, Northern Ireland and the UK have tried many times to find ways to stop 'the Troubles'. The 1994 ceasefire which followed the signing of the Downing Street Declaration in 1993 floundered with the IRA's bombing of Canary Wharf in London in 1996. Progress towards a final solution is slow and old attitudes on all sides die hard.

The facts outlined here may provide a little background to the current situation.

Ireland has been politically divided since 1920–1. After centuries of British rule, including a 120-year period when the whole of Ireland was governed as

Neoclassical Stormont – the former Northern Ireland Parliament building, Belfast part of the United Kingdom, 26 of its 32 counties gained their independence.

Six stayed out, forming Northern Ireland and remaining in the United Kingdom. They are Antrim, Armagh, Londonderry, Down, Fermanagh and Tyrone, in the Province of Ulster. The other counties of Ulster – Cavan, Donegal and Monaghan – are in the Republic of Ireland. The Constitution of Ireland and the Republic of Ireland Act (1949) severed Ireland's last formal links with Britain.

Northern Ireland elects 17 MPs to Parliament at Westminster. From 1921 to 1972, although Northern Ireland was represented at Westminster, the devolved Government at Stormont operated with virtual autonomy from London on local matters.

In 1972, as a result of increased IRA activity in Northern Ireland and paramilitary action by so-called Loyalist extremist groups, the British Government resumed direct responsibility for all aspects of the government of Northern Ireland. The Secretary of State for Northern Ireland is a member of the British Cabinet.

The Government of the Republic is a parliamentary democracy, with two Houses of Parliament – the Dáil, or House of Representatives, and the Seanad (Senate). The President is the head of state, and the Prime Minister (Taoiseach) is head of the Government. Where there is more than one candidate for the presidency, the President is elected by direct vote of the people.

The Constitution of Ireland, adopted by referendum in 1937, sets out the form of government, defining its powers and those of the President and Prime Minister. It also defines the structure and powers of the courts, sets out the

Leinster House is the seat of the Dáil (House of Representatives) and the Seanad (Senate)

fundamental rights of citizens and contains a number of directive principles of social policy.

The Dáil currently has 166 members, with six main political parties represented – Fianna Fáil, Fine Gael, Labour, Progressive Democrats, Democratic Left and the Workers' Party. The Seanad, with 60 members, may initiate or amend legislation.

Under the Constitution every citizen has the right to petition the courts to secure his or her rights or to have a judgement pronounced as to whether given legislation is compatible with the Constitution. Before signing a bill, the President may refer it to the Supreme Court for a decision on its compatibility with the Constitution. This procedure has led to a number of laws or parts of laws being declared unconstitutional and therefore void.

Local government, responsible for public housing, water and sanitation, road maintenance, vocational education and other services, is administered by 113 local authorities funded by state grants and local taxes on non-residential property.

Culture

*I*rish culture is a mystic blend of past and present, and the borders between myth and reality, magic and technology, absurdity and order are blurred. Legend merges into history, and myth becomes more tangible with the realisation that the places of legend actually exist.

Ireland's roots are firmly embedded in Celtic soil. The Celts, initially migrants, were an independent, imaginative people who loved a good song, a good story, a good argument and a good fight. Were? You will find them today – as proud of their heritage among the chic boutiques of Dublin's Grafton Street as they are on the windswept moorlands of Kerry and Connemara.

Signposts display names in both English and Irish, particularly in the Republic

The Celtic character has survived the violent prejudice of centuries. Oppression by the English, especially the 18th-century Penal Laws, stifled Irish culture and the Irish language almost to the point of extinction. Almost, but not quite.

Clandestine 'hedgerow schools' were set up, and when Ireland eventually became fully independent, Irish (Gaelic) was adopted as the first national language. It is now a compulsory subject in schools and is more widely spoken than at any time since the 19th century.

A major part of Britain's efforts to subjugate the Irish was the policy of 'plantation', under which Protestant migrants from England and Scotland were settled on lands confiscated from native Irish Catholics. Descendants of the Anglo-Irish Ascendancy, the privileged elite who controlled Ireland, still hold estates in the Republic. Caught between two worlds – an Irish homeland and an English heritage – they are treated with polite caution by their Irish neighbours, who still regard them as more English than the English.

Today, the Irish have regained a sense of identity that was almost lost forever, and Celtic pride is reflected in the traditional lettering on high street shop fronts, in literature, the arts and music.

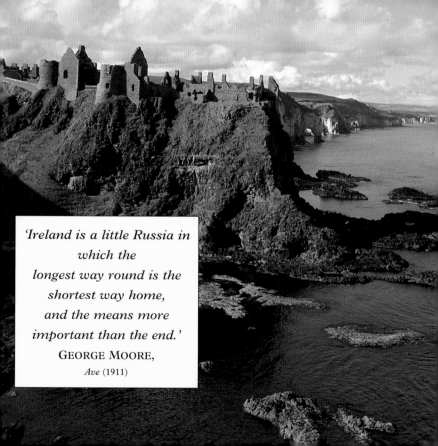

FIRST STEPS

'Ireland is a little Russia in which the longest way round is the shortest way home, and the means more important than the end.'
GEORGE MOORE,
Ave (1911)

ARRIVING
By air

There are five major international airports in Ireland: Shannon, Dublin, Cork, Knock and Belfast International at Aldergrove.

Shannon, on the west coast, is the gateway for flights from North America, but airline options for scheduled services are limited to Ireland's national carrier, Aer Lingus, and Delta. Flying via London opens up a much wider selection for travellers from Canada and the US.

Dublin Airport has good European connections. Aer Lingus, British Midland and Ryanair are the main carriers on routes between the UK and Ireland, while Aer Lingus and other major national airlines serve major European cities.

Cork Airport has direct flights to Dublin, London and limited continental destinations, with good connecting international flights through Dublin.

Knock Airport, Co Mayo, is officially known as Horan International Airport.

It owes its existence to the determination of a local priest who campaigned for years for an airport to serve the pilgrims who flock to the village where apparitions of the Virgin Mary were sighted in 1879. The airport has scheduled services from Britain, as well as international charter flights, and serves a large area of the northwest.

Belfast is served by two airports. Belfast International at Aldergrove, the principal gateway, is 30km from the city centre, but the motorway link is excellent. British Airways and British Midland Airways both run shuttle services between Aldergrove and London Heathrow. There are also connections with the other major British cities. Travellers from North America on scheduled flights are usually routed through London.

Belfast City Airport, only 7km from the city centre, receives flights from Luton Airport (about 30km from London), and from other UK provincial airports. (See **Arriving** pages 178–9.)

By sea

The only big ship that calls at Cobh, Co Cork, these days is the *QEII*, and then only once or twice a year. Travel by sea nowadays means a rather more prosaic crossing by car ferry from Britain or France.

The major routes to the Republic all start in Wales: Holyhead for Dun Laoghaire; Fishguard for Dun Laoghaire and Rosslare; Pembroke for Rosslare; and Swansea for Cork.

Belfast is served from the Scottish ports of Cairnryan and Stranraer, and from Liverpool. There are also services to Rosslare from Cherbourg and Le Havre, and to Cork from Le Havre and Roscoff. (See **Arriving** page 179.)

GETTING AROUND

Ireland is a small country (though probably much larger than most visitors expect) and communications are generally good.

By bus

Long distance services are operated by Bus Éireann in the Republic and Ulsterbus in Northern Ireland. Both offer a reasonably efficient and inexpensive method of travel, especially in areas infrequently serviced (or in some cases not served at all) by rail. City bus services, particularly in Dublin and Belfast, are excellent.

It is possible to travel between Britain and Ireland by bus – not the quickest way, but certainly economical. Services are operated by National Express-Supabus, based in Britain, and Slattery's, an Irish company. (See **Public Transport** page 187.)

By car

This is the best way of getting around Ireland. Roads are generally good – and getting better – on both sides of the border. The old image of the Irish road as a pot-holed ribbon of mud has long since given way to modern experience as improvement schemes, often funded by the European Union, speed ahead.

THOMAS COOK
Traveller's Tip
Any Thomas Cook Network location will offer airline ticket re-routing and re-validation free of charge to MasterCard holders and to travellers who have purchased their travel tickets from Thomas Cook.

By rail

Rail services in the Republic are operated by Irish Rail, the state-owned Irish Railway. Trains are comfortable and generally reliable and the fares reasonable. There are two classes of travel: standard (2nd class) and super-standard (1st class). Major towns and ports are easily reached from Dublin, but there are large gaps in the system, especially in the northwest.

Northern Ireland Railways, also state-owned, operates between Belfast and Londonderry, Bangor and Dublin. The Belfast-Dublin Express travels non-stop between the two cities in two hours. There are six trains a day in each direction, with a reduced service on Sundays. (See **Public Transport** page 187.)

Further details on rail services are contained in the *Thomas Cook European Timetable,* published monthly.

THE REGIONS

Ireland's ancient provinces – Ulster, Munster, Leinster and Connacht – roughly divide the country into north, south, east and west.

Ulster is an unbelievably beautiful region. North of Belfast, the Antrim Coast Road, leading to the Giant's Causeway, is unquestionably one of the world's most beautiful coastal routes, presenting a kaleidoscope of picturesque glens, villages and fishing harbours. For mountain-lovers there are the Mountains of Mourne, sweeping down to the sea in Co Down, and the Sperrins in Co Tyrone. The Fermanagh Lakelands are a Valhalla for boaters and anglers.

Munster extends southwards from Galway Bay to Mizen Head and the island of Cape Clear, and eastwards to Waterford. Soaring cliffs punctuate a coastline of rocky coves and soft, sandy beaches. Here are the ancient places: Viking Limerick and Waterford; the forts of Dingle Peninsula; and the legendary Rock of Cashel.

Leinster stretches from the border of Ulster south to Co Wexford, and from the Irish Sea to the River Shannon. Here the clan rulers built the great burial mound at Newgrange, and later the High Kings of Ireland ruled from the Hill of Tara. Brian Ború defeated the Vikings at Clontarf, near Dublin, in 1014, and in 1690 William of Orange's victory at the Battle of the Boyne set up a chain of events that continues to the present day.

Connacht, the far west of Ireland, is a land of wide horizons with mountains brooding over the ever-changing Atlantic Ocean on one side and the fertile plains of the Shannon Valley on the other. To the south, medieval Galway City gazes out towards the Aran Isles, and in the north Benbulben dominates Sligo and the landscapes that inspired W B Yeats.

Jaunting car, ideal for getting about

THE BORDER

The border between the Republic and Northern Ireland, created in 1921 by Britain's Government of Ireland Act, loops from the western shore of Lough Foyle to Carlingford Lough, just south of Newry, Co Down.

Under the Act, six of Ulster's nine counties – Antrim, Armagh, Down, Fermanagh, Londonderry and Tyrone – were retained as part of the United Kingdom. Cavan, Donegal and Monaghan, part of the Republic, are the remaining counties.

The border left a number of communities effectively straddling two jurisdictions – no problem during peaceful times (apart from creating opportunities for smuggling), but a security hazard when violence arose.

Now the border stands as a symbol of a divided Ireland, and it underscores the ambivalence implied in the North by the question, 'Are you British or are you Irish?'. The people of Northern Ireland can choose between an Irish or British passport – many pragmatists carry both. The removal of customs and immigration barriers in the European Union has effectively removed frontiers between member-states, but has made little difference to the mental divide between north and south in Ireland.

In terms of everyday travel, however, the border has never been a truly formidable frontier. Even at the height of the Troubles, when British Army patrols were much in evidence and drivers had to zig-zag through barbed-wire barriers, the business of passing from one country to another was completed with little of the formality and tension found in other parts of the world.

Statue of William of Orange, who landed at Carrickfergus in 1690

The casual nature of the border is underscored by the Shannon-Erne Waterway, which traverses counties Leitrim, Cavan and Fermanagh to link the rivers Shannon and Erne. Opened in 1993, the restored waterway flits back and forth across the border – and is itself the border in some places – but nowhere along its 63km length is there a checkpoint or Customs post; instead the waterway is occupied only by boats and pleasure cruisers.

LIFESTYLE AND ETIQUETTE

A modern phrase sums up perfectly a lifestyle which has prevailed in Ireland since the first Celtic herdsman reclined on the turf with a happy sigh. The phrase is 'laid back'.

Time, they will tell you in Ireland, is the one asset each of us has in equal measure: 24 hours of it replenished every single day. Most of us treat it like money – budgeting it, counting it, auditing it, and trying to make a profit from it. The Irish regard it as part of their heritage; an heirloom to be cherished like a work of art. Time is too precious to be squandered on mundane commerce.

A conversation struck up with a fellow passenger on a

Time to stand and watch the world

bus can have either or both of you missing the stop.

A visit to the pub can extend well beyond the limit you set yourself, for there is no such thing in Ireland as a quick drink. Warmly, easily, you are drawn into the conversation, questioned but not cross-examined, listened to with

Dublin's Abbey Theatre is famous for plays by Irish writers about the Irish

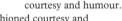

courtesy and humour.

Old-fashioned courtesy and hospitality thrive in Ireland. Men still hold doors open for women and give up their seats for them on buses and trains – though the obverse of that coin is an equally old-fashioned chauvinism.

The basic rule for visitors is: 'Be garrulous.' When you are addressed do reply, and fully. Better still, get in first with a greeting and a comment on the weather. But never initiate discussion on issues the Irish are particularly sensitive about – especially abortion, divorce, religion and The North.

WHAT TO SEE

Leinster

*L*einster is a province of varied and lovely scenery, with fascinating bogland, fish-filled lakes, the River Shannon, nature reserves, sandy beaches, stately homes and castles. There are more counties here than the other three provinces – 12 of the 32 – plus the Republic's capital, Dublin.

DUBLIN CITY
ABBEY THEATRE
Founded in 1904 by W B Yeats and friends for the performance of plays by and about the Irish – Yeats, Synge, Shaw, O'Casey and others have had plays premièred here (see page 58). It incorporates the smaller Peacock Theatre.
Lower Abbey Street, Dublin 1.
Tel: 01–878 7222.

BANK OF IRELAND
This magnificent 18th-century building, with its huge multi-coloured porticoes and sculptured figures, was originally designed as the Irish Parliament House.

The exquisite Chinese ceiling in the Chester Beatty Library and Gallery of Oriental Art

When Parliament ceased to exist after the Act of Union in 1800, the Bank of Ireland bought the building. The former House of Commons can be seen. Groups can also arrange to see the House of Lords, still in its original form.
College Green, Dublin 2. Tel: 01–677 6801. Open: Monday to Friday 10am–4pm (to 5pm Thursday). Free.

CHESTER BEATTY LIBRARY AND GALLERY OF ORIENTAL ART
Donated to the country by Sir Alfred Chester Beatty (1875–1968), exhibits include manuscripts ranging from biblical papyri to Persian Korans, prints, wall hangings and Oriental artefacts.
20 Shrewsbury Road, Ballsbridge, Dublin 4. Tel: 01–269 2386. Open: Tuesday to Friday 10am–5pm, Saturday 2.30–5pm. Free guided tours Wednesdays and Saturdays 2.30pm.

CHRIST CHURCH CATHEDRAL
This historic Church of Ireland (Anglican) cathedral was founded in 1038 by Sitric Silkenbeard, King of the Dublin Norsemen, who built a simple wooden church here. It was later rebuilt in stone by Richard de Clare, Earl of Pembroke (Strongbow) in 1169. There is a monument to Strongbow in the south aisle (see page 57).
Christ Church Place, Dublin 8. Tel: 01–677 8099. Open: daily 10am–5pm. Donation appreciated.

CITY HALL

The seat of Dublin Corporation since 1852, City Hall was built between 1769 and 1779 as the Royal Exchange. It was the scene of the Irish Volunteer rallies in the 1780s, and Government troops used it as a barracks and torture chamber during the 1798 rebellion. It has a beautiful domed entrance hall.
Dame Street, Dublin 2. Tel: 01–679 6111.
Open: Monday to Friday 9am–1pm,
2.15–5pm. Free.

LEINSTER

CIVIC MUSEUM

Devoted to the history of local commerce, industry, transport and politics, exhibits include coins from the Dublin Vikings' mint, flint axes, old maps and views of Dublin. Exhibitions on Dublin life are held periodically.
58 South William Street, Dublin 2. Tel: 01–679 4260. Open: Tuesday to Saturday 10am–6pm, Sunday 11am–2pm. Free.

CUSTOM HOUSE

Although not open to the public, the commanding exterior of the Custom House warrants more than a passing glance from the far side of the Talbot Memorial Bridge. This 18th-century Liffey-side building, designed by James Gandon, was set on fire by nationalist forces in 1921 and severely damaged. Major restoration took place in the late 1980s (see page 58).
Custom House Quay, Dublin 2.

DUBLIN CASTLE

Built in the early 13th century, only one of the four Norman towers – the Record Tower – survives. Presidents of Ireland have been inaugurated in lofty St Patrick's Hall since 1938, and foreign dignitaries are hosted in the elegant State Apartments (see page 57).

Dame Street, Dublin 2. Tel: 01–677 7129. Open: Monday to Friday 10am–12.15pm, 2–5pm, weekends 2–5pm. Times may vary because of state functions – check with the Tourist Information Centre (tel: 01–679 2777). Admission charge.

DUBLIN EXPERIENCE

This multi-media interpretation of Dublin and its people from the 10th century to modern times is a useful and entertaining 45-minute presentation, best seen before sightseeing.
Thomas Davis Theatre, Trinity College Campus, Dublin 2. Tel: 01–677 2941, ext 1177. Open: late May to early October, daily 10am–5pm. Admission charge.

DUBLIN WRITERS' MUSEUM

Opened in 1991, the museum has paintings and busts of many of Dublin's major writers, as well as memorabilia and rare books. There is a lecture theatre, temporary exhibitions, a children's book section and a centre where Irish authors can meet, carry

Sumptuous furnishings for the State Drawing Rooms in Dublin Castle

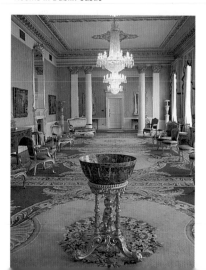

out research and work (see page 59).
18–19 Parnell Square North, Dublin 1.
Tel: 01–872 2077. Open: Monday to
Saturday 10am–5pm, Sunday and public
holidays 2–6pm. Admission charge.

DUBLIN ZOO

Open for over 160 years, this is one of
the few zoos where lions have bred in
captivity, one achieving worldwide fame
as the MGM film lion. There is a large
collection of wild animals and birds,
some endangered, from many countries,
as well as information panels, a pets'
corner and a train ride around the zoo.
Phoenix Park, Dublin 7. Tel: 01–677 1425.
Open: daily 9.30am–6pm. Admission charge.

FOUR COURTS

Architect James Gandon produced a
masterpiece with this building, opened
in 1802, which houses the law courts of
Chancery, King's Bench, Exchequer and
Common Pleas. It was badly damaged
in 1922, at the outbreak of civil war; a
three-day battle ended with an explosion
destroying many of Ireland's historical
records and official deeds (see page 59).
Inns Quay, Dublin 8. Tel: 01–872 5555.
Open: Monday to Friday 11am–1pm,
2–4pm. Free.

GENERAL POST OFFICE

The imposing GPO building, with its
Ionic portico and fluted pillars, was
completed in 1818 and virtually
destroyed in the Easter Rising of 1916
(see page 59). It reopened in 1929.
Inside is a bronze statue of the dying
Cuchulainn, leader of the Red Branch
Knights in Irish mythology .
O'Connell Street, Dublin 1. Tel: 01–872
8888. Open: Monday to Saturday
8am–8pm, Sunday and public holidays
10.30am–6.30pm.

GUINNESS HOP STORE VISITOR CENTRE

A cooperage display and transport
gallery relating to the Guinness Empire
are housed in a four-storey, 19th-
century Hop Store on the brewery's
original 26-hectare site. The World of
Guinness exhibition includes an audio-
visual presentation showing the history
and manufacture of Dublin's most
famous product. There are no public
tours of the brewery but Guinness can
be sampled at the Hop Store bar.
Crane Street (off Thomas Street),
Dublin 8. Tel: 01–453 6700. Open:
Monday to Friday 10am–4pm (excluding
public holidays). Admission charge.

The 'Cooper' demonstrates his skills at the
World of Guinness exhibition

TOWN LIFE

A town, the dictionaries say, is a place with a large number of dwellings; a densely populated settlement with a concentration of commerce. The word implies an increased pace, sophistication and a degree of stress.

In Ireland, still largely rural in spite of shopping malls, leisure centres and EU-funded highways, a town is often best described as a coming together of pubs around a square in which one may trade on market days and gossip the whole year round.

Many of the larger towns are still small enough for the surrounding countryside – the fields, forests and mountains – to be visible from their centres. Even in metropolitan Dublin the eye can move in a single sweep from a group of dinner-jacketed, ball-gowned students crossing Grafton Street after an all-night party to a man decorously clad in tweed suit and green wellington boots.

The closeness of the land to Irish town life is underscored by the greengrocers' stores, often quite small places with rough-and-ready displays of fruit and vegetables – slightly battered-looking apples, carrots with the earth still clinging – and an absence of plastic pre-packaging. Everything looks as if it has been harvested just down the road, as indeed it probably has.

There is a delightfully old-fashioned ambience: crowded hardware store windows filled with unidentifiable – often indescribable – bits and pieces of

Street life and street character

agricultural and horticultural bric-à-brac; elderly people sedately pedalling along on heavy old bicycles; dogs roaming freely; uniformed school-children; and housewives chatting on doorsteps.

And there are those things which make it all uniquely Irish: Gaelic lettering over the shop fronts; handmade posters advertising a *ceilidh* (pronounced kay-lee), perhaps, or a visiting storyteller; and the versatility of Irish business people who can combine an estate agency with a tea shop, or a pub with a funeral parlour.

IRISH WHISKEY CORNER

Part of the old Jameson's Distillery complex, built in 1791 and converted into the head offices of Irish Distillers when several companies merged, houses this museum which includes an audio-visual presentation and a sampling of the goods in the Ball o' Malt Bar (see page 59).
Bow Street, Dublin 7. Tel: 01–872 5566. Tours: 3.30pm weekdays. Admission charge.

JAMES JOYCE CULTURAL CENTRE

The literary display in this impressive Georgian house includes biographies of characters from *Ulysses* based on Dublin people whom Joyce knew. Walking tours of the author's Dublin are organised.
35 North Great George's Street, Dublin 1. Tel: 01–873 1984. Open: Monday to Saturday 10am–4.30pm, Sunday 12.30–4.30pm. Admission charge.

KILMAINHAM GAOL

History covering an eventful century and a half is almost tangible at Kilmainham Gaol, erected in 1796. Now a museum pinpointing Irish political and penal history from the 1780s to the 1920s, the old gaol still presents a gruesome atmosphere.

Eamonn de Valera, former leader of Fianna Fáil, Taoiseach (Prime Minister), and later President, was one of the last prisoners to be held here. Years later, in 1966, he officially declared open the Kilmainham Gaol Museum.

A fascinating audio-visual presentation gives a 30-minute outline of Irish nationalism over a 200-year period.
Inchicore Road, Dublin 8. Tel: 01–453 5984. Open: June to September, daily 10am–6pm; October to May, Wednesday and Sunday only 2–6pm. Admission charge.

LEINSTER HOUSE

The Dáil (lower house) and Seanad (senate) of the Irish Parliament meet in this lavish building, constructed in 1745 as the town house of the Dukes of Leinster, but to enter the Visitors' Gallery you need an introduction from a Teachta Dáil (MP).
Kildare Street, Dublin 2.

Exhibits at Kilmainham Gaol evoke the bleak reality of a term of imprisonment

KILMAINHAM'S INMATES

Eamonn de Valera, born in New York of Irish ancestry, strongly influenced Irish politics over a long period. His spell in gaol was for his part in the 1916 Easter Rising; he was released in 1924. One of de Valera's predecessors in Kilmainham was Home Rule Party leader Charles Stewart Parnell. Leaders of the Easter Rising were executed at the gaol, among them Con Colbert, Padraig Pearse and James Connolly.

THE LIBERTIES

This area in the southwest of the city covers around 80 hectares. Historically, the name originates from privileges bestowed under Magna Carta. Today it is an interesting precinct of markets, bargain shops, betting shops, churches and pubs.

MARSH'S LIBRARY

Opened in 1707, this is Ireland's oldest public library. Inside are 'cages' in which readers were locked to prevent theft. *St Patrick's Close, Dublin 8. Tel: 01–454 3511. Open: Monday, Wednesday to Friday 10am–12.45pm, 2–5pm, Saturday 10.30am–12.45pm. Donation appreciated.*

DUBLIN

MUSEUM OF CHILDHOOD

This fascinating little museum includes collections of dolls from 1730 to 1940, dolls' prams, dolls' houses, rocking horses and miniature furniture, as well as a wide range of other toys.
The Palms, 20 Palmerston Park, Rathmines, Dublin 6. Tel: 01–497 3223. Open: July and August, Wednesday and Sunday 2–5.30pm; rest of year, Sunday only 2–5.30pm. Admission charge.

NATIONAL BOTANIC GARDENS

Twenty thousand different plant species are set in 20 hectares of rock, herb and rose gardens and herbaceous borders, and in the superb mid-19th-century glasshouses, designed and built by Richard Turner. The gardens, in their attractive setting beside the River Tolka, date from 1795.
Glasnevin, Dublin 9. Tel: 01–837 7596. Open: summer, Monday to Saturday 9am–6pm, Sunday 11am–6pm; winter, Monday to Saturday 10am–4.30pm, Sunday 11am–4.30pm (greenhouses open for fewer hours). Free.

NATIONAL GALLERY

The gallery houses Ireland's foremost collection of paintings, including works by Rembrandt, Reynolds, El Greco and Goya. Every major European school of painting is represented among the 2,400 paintings, 5,200 drawings, watercolours and miniatures and 3,000 prints. Vestments, objets d'art and 300 pieces of sculpture are also exhibited. Irish painters are strongly represented, with works by George Barrett, Francis Danby and James Latham, among others.
Merrion Square West, Dublin 2. Tel: 01–661 5133. Open: Monday to Saturday 10am–5.30pm (to 8.30pm Thursday), Sunday 2–5pm. Free.

NATIONAL LIBRARY

This treasure-house of information about Ireland has many books, including first editions, complete files of Irish magazines and newspapers, maps, prints, drawings and photographs. Tickets are issued for reading the books.
Kildare Street, Dublin 2. Tel: 01–661 8811. Open: Monday 10am–9pm, Tuesday and Wednesday 2–9pm, Thursday and Friday 10am–5pm, Saturday 10am–1pm. Free.

NATIONAL MUSEUM

Opened in 1890, the museum was the result of merging several collections. It

The National Gallery is a treasure house of European and Irish artwork

comprises the Irish Antiquities, Art and Natural History divisions, and contains artefacts and masterpieces dating from the first century AD to the 16th century. Among notable exhibits are the 8th-century Ardagh Chalice, and the 12th-century Cross of Cong. The music room includes a display of Irish harps.

Kildare Street, Merrion Row and Merrion Street, Dublin 2. Tel: 01–677 7444. Open: Tuesday to Saturday 10am–5pm (from 10.30am Friday), Sunday 2–5pm. Free but a charge for specialist exhibitions.

NATIONAL WAX MUSEUM

Among life-size Irish historical, political and literary figures in wax are Irish and international stars from the worlds of sport and entertainment. Exhibitions include Children's World of Fairytale and Fantasy, the Hall of Megastars, a replica of da Vinci's *Last Supper*, and a Chamber of Horrors (see page 59).

Granby Row, off Parnell Square, Dublin 1. Tel: 01–872 6340. Open: Monday to Saturday 10am–5.30pm, Sunday noon–5.30pm. Admission charge.

NATURAL HISTORY MUSEUM

This zoological museum has a large collection of the vertebrate and invertebrate wildlife of Ireland. As well as mammals, birds, butterflies and other insects, fish, fowl and mammals from Africa and Asia are displayed, including skeletons of prehistoric animals.

Merrion Street, Dublin 2. Tel: 01–677 7444. Open: Tuesday to Saturday 10am–5pm (from 10.30am Friday), Sunday 2–5pm. Free.

PHOENIX PARK

One of the largest enclosed public parks in the world with 710 hectares, Phoenix

Delightful walk along the River Tolka at the National Botanic Gardens

Park was laid out in the 18th century. Its name (*fionn uisce*) means 'clear water'. It contains lakes, gardens, woods, a herd of deer and a zoo (see page 27), with space for soccer, Gaelic football, hurling, cricket and polo. The residences of the Irish President and the US Ambassador, and the headquarters of the Garda (police), with a small police museum, are also in the park. The Ashtown Castle Visitors' Centre houses interpretative displays, an exhibition area, audio-visual room and a restaurant.

West of Heuston Station, Dublin 8. Open: daily. Police museum – tel: 01–677 1156. Open: Monday to Friday 9am–5pm. Free.

POWERSCOURT TOWNHOUSE CENTRE

Converted in the 1980s into a highly sophisticated, traffic-free precinct of select shops, cafés, craft shops and boutiques, these former wholesale textile company's premises were originally built between 1771 and 1774 as the town mansion of the Powerscourt family. The HQ Gallery, the Craft Council of Ireland's showroom for Irish craft and design, is located here.

South William Street, Dublin 2. Open: daily 9am–6pm, except Sunday and public holidays. HQ Gallery – tel: 01–679 7368. Open: Monday 10am–5pm, Tuesday to Saturday 10am–6pm. Free.

ROYAL CANAL

A pleasant waterway with more than 11km of towpath winding through northern Dublin, the Royal Canal never reached its full potential as a cargo-carrying connection between the Liffey and the Shannon; the Grand Canal, passing through the city's southern suburbs, was already doing that. Long John Binns, a shoemaker, founded The Royal as a rival waterway in 1789. It lost money from the start, though the canal endures to this day as a leisure attraction. Some still call it the Shoemaker's Canal.

ROYAL HOSPITAL

Kilmainham's Royal Hospital is Ireland's only surviving fully classical 17th-century building. It was designed by William Robinson in the 1680s to house retired and disabled soldiers. It officially passed to the Irish Free State in 1922, and subsequently became the headquarters of the Garda (Irish police). Extensive restorations were carried out in 1980. The government designated the building the National Centre for Culture and the Arts and its interior is considered among the finest in Dublin. It houses the Irish Museum of Modern Art, whose excellent displays of international art include works by Picasso, and Irish art of the 20th century. In the grounds are two cemeteries: one is believed to contain the body of Irish patriot Robert Emmet who led the 1803 rising and was executed. British soldiers who died in the 1916 rising occupy the other, along with army pensioners.

Kilmainham Lane, Dublin 8. Tel: 01–671 8666. Hospital – open: July and August, Tuesday to Sunday noon–5pm; rest of year, Tuesday to Saturday 2–5pm. Free, but a charge may be made for special events. Museum – open: Tuesday to Saturday 10am–5.30pm, Sunday noon–5.30pm.

For over 240 years – until 1927 – generations of old soldiers were residents at the Royal Hospital, Kilmainham

James Joyce

*J*ames Joyce, one of Ireland's greatest writers, spent most of his life outside the country, but he wrote only about Dublin and Dubliners. He knew the city so well and used its detail so minutely in his works, that it was claimed if Dublin were to be totally destroyed, his novel *Ulysses* could be used as a blueprint to rebuild it.

Born in 1882 at 41 Brighton Square, in Rathgar, 5km from the city centre, Joyce lived at more than 20 other addresses before leaving Dublin at the age of 22. After that he wrote about the city as he travelled abroad.

Between 1893 and 1898 he attended Belvedere College in Great Denmark Street before studying at University College Dublin. At 35 North Great George's Street is the James Joyce Cultural Centre (see page 30) whose library and archives attract serious students of the writer and his work.

Each year, 16 June – the day on which the whole action of *Ulysses* takes place – sees special Bloomsday events throughout the city and at the Ormond Hotel on Upper Ormond Quay, a meeting place for Leopold Bloom, the principal character in the book.

Bronze statue of Joyce in honour of his famous novel *Ulysses*

A short walk from the eastern end of Railway Street is the DART system's Connolly Station, from where Joyce fans can take a train two stops to Pearse Station, south of the Liffey. Just outside the station is Westland Row, at the end of which is Sweny's Pharmacy, remaining much as it is described in *Ulysses*.

Sandymount Strand, a 5km beach between Ringsend and Booterstown, is another *Ulysses* setting and was a favourite spot with Joyce and his wife, Nora Barnacle. The Martello tower at Dun Laoghaire, featured in the first chapter of *Ulysses,* is now a Joyce museum (see page 44).

LITERARY IRELAND

No other small country has produced as many big names in the world of literature as Ireland – names that confront the visitor in each of the ancient provinces.

Dublin has so many associations with literature that in 1991 it opened a Writers' Museum at 18–19 Parnell Square North (see page 26).

Lovers of James Joyce can follow the steps of his *Ulysses* character, Leopold Bloom, through the streets of Dublin and visit the Martello tower at Sandycove (see page 44), where the author lived for a short time. As a young man, the dramatist George Bernard Shaw lived briefly with his family at Torca Cottage, up nearby Dalkey Hill.

Jonathan Swift, author of *Gulliver's Travels*, is buried in Dublin's St Patrick's Cathedral, where he served as Dean from 1713 to 1745. Swift attended Kilkenny College, where playwrights William Congreve and George Farquhar also studied.

Edith Somerville and Violet Martin Ross, the authors of the hilarious *Experiences of an Irish RM*, lived in Castletownshend, near Skibbereen, Co Cork. They are buried in the cemetery of St Barrahane's Church.

The Yeats Trail through Sligo and Leitrim is a 160km signposted tour through locations immortalised by the poet W B Yeats and his artist brother Jack.

Ulster also has its share of great names. Oscar Wilde and Samuel Beckett were pupils at Portora Royal School, Enniskillen. Louis MacNeice grew up at Carrickfergus overlooking Belfast Lough and C S Lewis was

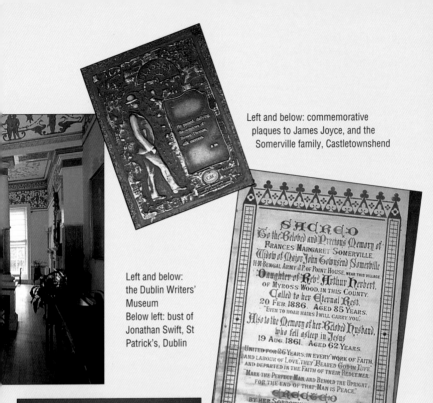

Left and below: commemorative plaques to James Joyce, and the Somerville family, Castletownshend

Left and below: the Dublin Writers' Museum
Below left: bust of Jonathan Swift, St Patrick's, Dublin

a Belfast man. But the province is best known now for its contemporary writers – such names as Benedict Kelly, John Montague and Seamus Heaney.

Irish Literature dates from about AD600. It was exposed to European influences by such modern writers as Pádraic Pearse (1879–1916) and Pádraic Ó Conaire (1883–1928). Among other distinguished writers in Irish were Liam O Flaitheartaigh (O'Flaherty) and Brendan Behan.

ST ANNE'S PARK ROSE GARDEN

A mecca for the rose specialist in the centre of Dublin Corporation's public park, the gardens were created in conjunction with Clontarf Horticultural Society. More than 100 numbered and catalogued varieties of floribunda, hybrid tea, old shrub roses and miniatures bloom in summer.

Clontarf, Dublin 3 (off the Howth road). Guided tours available by arrangement with the Parks Department (tel: 01–833 1941), or Clontarf Horticultural Society (tel: 01–872 1076). Open at all times.

ST AUDOEN'S CHURCH OF IRELAND (Anglican)

One of the oldest churches in Dublin, near a preserved stretch of the city wall and minus much of its roof, St Audoen's is dated variously from AD650 to 1169. A pre-Norse church of St Columcille once stood on the site. The tower contains three bells cast in 1423, said to be the oldest in Ireland. In the porch is an early Christian gravestone, known as the 'Lucky Stone', which has been kept at the church since before 1309 (see page 57).

High Street, Dublin 8.

Detailed wood carving on St Michan's organ, which dates from around 1725

ST AUDOEN'S ROMAN CATHOLIC CHURCH

Next door to St Audoen's Church of Ireland, is the Roman Catholic church, dating from the 1840s. 'The Flame on the Hill', an audio-visual presentation telling the story of the history of Christianity in Ireland, is shown at the church.

High Street, Dublin 8. Open: daily 10am–4.30pm. Admission charge.

ST MICHAN'S CHURCH

The original 1095 Danish church was almost completely rebuilt in the 1680s and restored in the 19th century. The finely carved 18th-century organ in the Anglican church is believed to have been played by Handel while composing *The Messiah* in the year which saw its first public performance at Neale's New Music Hall in Fishamble Street. Probably the main 'attraction' at St Michan's is a tour of the vaults, where a number of corpses, some from the 17th century, can be viewed in an extraordinarily well-preserved state (see page 59).

Lower Church Street, Dublin 8. Tel: 01–872 4154. Open: Monday to Friday 10am–12.45pm, 2–4.45pm, Saturday 10am–12.45pm. Donation appreciated.

ST PATRICK'S CATHEDRAL

St Patrick is said to have baptised converts to the Christian faith in a well which once existed adjacent to the present National Cathedral of the Church of Ireland. Because of the sacred association with St Patrick, a church has stood here since the 5th century. A Norman church was built on the site in 1190, and re-building took place in the first half of the 13th century, resulting in the magnificent edifice which exists today. Jonathan Swift, Dean of St Patrick's for more than 30 years, is buried in the nave, and there is a marble bust of him in the south aisle (see page 57).

Patrick Street, Dublin 8. Tel: 01–475 4817. Open: Monday to Friday 9am–6pm, Saturday 9am–5pm (4pm November to March), Sunday 10am–4.30pm. Admission charge.

Above: St Patrick's Cathedral was extensively restored in the 1860s

Left: paper marbling – one of a wide range of crafts at Tower Design

TOWER DESIGN GUILD

Heraldic artistry, silk painting, wood carving, pewter engineering, etching, pottery and designer knitting are among the crafts which can be seen here. A shop sells a range of craft products.

IDA Enterprise Centre, Pearse Street, Dublin 2. Tel: 01–677 5655. Open: Monday to Friday 8.30am–5.30pm, some units closed 1–2pm. Shop: Monday to Friday 10am–5pm. Free.

WATERWAYS VISITOR CENTRE

Through exhibition material and audio-visual facilities, this fascinating and informative centre interprets the historical role of Ireland's navigable waterways over the years, and their development into a valuable public amenity.

Grand Canal Basin, Ringsend, Dublin 2. Tel: 01–661 3111. Open: daily 9.30am–6pm. Admission charge.

Trinity College

*O*ne of Dublin's three universities, Trinity is situated in busy College Green in the heart of the city. It was built on the site of an Augustinian Priory, All Hallows. Through the great arched gate, with its statues of two famous graduates, Oliver Goldsmith and Edmund Burke, is a spacious area of lawns and cobbled squares, and gardens surrounded by buildings of various architectural styles and periods. The oldest part of the college is the Rubrics, a row of red-brick buildings dating from 1700.

Queen Elizabeth I founded Trinity College, the sole college of Dublin University, in 1592 as a seat of learning and the establishment of 'true religion' within the realm. Protestantism was the religion she had in mind, and for centuries Catholics were prohibited from Trinity.

Today, Trinity College caters for around 8,000 students, following in the footsteps of such illustrious literary giants as Jonathan Swift, Samuel Beckett, Oscar Wilde and Bram Stoker. Women students have been admitted since 1903.

The tall campanile near the centre of Library Square was erected in 1852. Beyond it, screened by gracious maple trees and old lamps, is the famous library which houses many ancient

Sculpture outside Trinity's Library

St Patrick's Day Parade, 17 March, is celebrated in style in Dublin

ST PATRICK

St Patrick's Day, 17 March, is marked in Ireland, the United States and other parts of the world with parades and cheering crowds. But the carnival spirit is a fairly recent development, evolved mainly in North America. Once, St Patrick's Day in Ireland was a very sombre affair, with the pubs closed and parades of industrial floats – more in line with the hair-shirt zeal of the saint and his contemporaries.

Born in the west of Roman Britain about AD389, Patrick led a restless life. As a boy he was captured by Irish pirates and taken to Co Antrim, where he was sold into slavery. After six years he escaped, trained as a missionary and returned to Ireland 37 years later. He dedicated the rest of his life – some sources say he reached the age of 104 – to challenging the druids and converting the kings of Ireland to Christianity. Until the late 17th century the Irish never used Patrick as a first name out of respect. Now one in four males is named after him.

volumes in the Long Room, including the oldest of them all – the *Book of Kells*.

The Long Room itself warrants inspection, with its barrel-vaulted ceiling 12.5m high, and tall shelves of leather-bound books, many of them accessible only by narrow ladder (but not by the public). Altogether, Trinity has more than two and a half million books.

To the right of the entrance to the college is the Examination Hall, a former theatre. Its massive blackened doors must have struck terror in the heart of many a candidate. The hall is sometimes used for concerts. Like the Chapel opposite, which is shared by all Christian

THE *BOOK OF KELLS*

The *Book of Kells* is a richly coloured, minutely detailed version of the Gospels, written in Latin on vellum. Originally one volume, the vast book, now regarded as one of the world's finest illuminated manuscripts, was divided into four when repairs were carried out in the 1950s. Two of these, opened at intricately decorated pages, can be closely examined by visitors (but be prepared for crowds).

denominations, it has a barrel-vaulted ceiling and notable plasterwork. Near the Chapel is the college Dining Hall, which sometimes doubles as an examination room.

If Trinity seems familiar, you may perhaps recognise it from the campus scenes in the 1983 film, *Educating Rita*. *College Green, Dublin 2. Tel: 01–608 2320. Grounds – open: daily 8am–10pm. Freely accessible. Library – open: Monday to Friday 9.30am–4.45pm, Saturday 9.30am–12.45pm. Admission charge, except for students under 18.*

Fine plants and wide views at Fernhill Gardens, renowned for their camellias and rhododendrons

CO DUBLIN
BEECH PARK
Beech Park's unique collection of herbaceous and alpine plants, some very rare, is set in the old walled garden of a Regency house, and includes woodland plants, New Zealand daisies and a Georgian hothouse used for propagation.
Clonsilla. Tel: 01–821 2216. Open: March to October, first weekend of every month 2–6pm; July and August, every Sunday and public holidays. Admission charge.

CASINO
About 5km north of Dublin, off the Malahide Road, this 18th-century former summerhouse – not a casino in the gambling sense – is in the Palladian style. Pillars, stone lions and balustrades provide generous ornamentation, while inside there are elaborate plaster ceilings. Built for the 1st Earl of Charlemont, the Casino was restored in the early 1980s.

Malahide Road, Marino. Tel: 01–833 1618. Open: June to September, daily 10am–6.30pm. Admission charge.

DRIMNAGH CASTLE
On the southwestern outskirts of Dublin, Drimnagh is the only Irish castle retaining a flooded moat, where up to 20 species of fowl live. It has a restored great hall, a battlement tower with look-out posts, stables, a coach house, a folly tower and gardens laid out in formal 17th-century style.
Longanile Road, Dublin 12. Tel: 01–453 5984. Open: mid–April to October, Wednesday, Saturday and Sunday 10am–5pm. Admission charge.

FERNHILL GARDENS
These 100-hectare privately owned gardens are renowned for their camellias, rhododendrons, magnolias and azaleas. There is also a fine collection of trees more than 200 years old, a meadow filled with wild flowers and a Victorian kitchen garden.

Sandyford. Tel: 01–295 6000. Open: March to November, Tuesday, Saturday and public holidays 11am–5pm, Sunday 2–6pm. Admission charge.

FRY MODEL RAILWAY

This museum shows not only scale models of Irish trains dating from 1832 to Dublin's modern DART system, but also an intriguing layout which includes the River Liffey, the Hill of Howth and other local landscapes.

Malahide Castle, Malahide. Tel: 01–846 3779. Open: Monday to Friday 10am–5pm, Saturday 11am–6pm, Sunday 2–6pm. Admission charge.

HOWTH CASTLE GARDENS

The gardens, adjoining the Deerpark Hotel and Golf Course, are best visited in May and early June. Started in 1854, they are famous for their rhododendrons – several thousands of them. Within the estate are the ruins of 16th-century Corr Castle and a neolithic dolmen known as Aideen's Grave. The oldest part of Howth Castle dates from 1464, but it has been altered in every century since. The castle is closed to the public, but admission to the gardens is free.

Howth Castle, Howth. Tel: 01–832 2624. Open: daily 8am–sunset.

DUBLIN ENVIRONS

HOWTH TRANSPORT MUSEUM

This small museum exhibits early fire engines, trucks, tractors and other vehicles. The Hill of Howth No 9 train and a Giant's Causeway tram are among the stars of the show.
Howth Castle, Howth. Tel: 01–847 5623/ 848 0831. Open: Saturday, Sunday and public holidays 2–6pm. Admission charge.

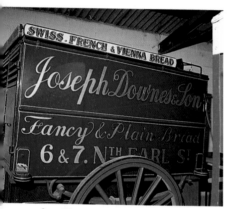

One of the many superbly restored exhibits at Howth Transport Museum

JAMES JOYCE TOWER AND MUSEUM

The Martello tower where Joyce spent a few weeks in 1904 as a guest of Oliver St John Gogarty is featured in his novel *Ulysses*, with Gogarty as the character of Buck Mulligan. Built in 1804, the tower contains a selection of Joyce memorabilia – the piano and guitar he played, a cigar case, a cane, manuscripts and a death mask of the author cast on 13 January 1941.
Sandycove, Dun Laoghaire. Tel: 01– 280 9265/872 2077. Open: April to October, Monday to Saturday 10am– 1pm, 2–5pm, Sunday 2–6pm. By appointment in winter. Admission charge.

MALAHIDE CASTLE

Except for a brief period when Cromwell evicted them, the Talbot family lived here continuously from 1185 to 1976, when Dublin County Council bought the property. The Great Hall, which has a minstrels' gallery, contains many portraits, while the Oak Room and two drawing rooms contain 17th-, 18th- and 19th-century furniture. The castle has an antiques shop and there are picnic areas in the grounds.
Malahide. Tel: 01–846 2184. Open: all year, Monday to Friday 10am–12.45pm, 2–5pm; April to October, Saturday 11am–6pm, Sunday and public holidays 2–6pm; November to March, Saturday, Sunday and public holidays 2–5pm. Admission charge.

NATIONAL MARITIME MUSEUM OF IRELAND

Housed in the 1837 Mariners' Church, this museum has, among many exhibits, an 11m French longboat captured in Bantry Bay in 1796, and a noted collection of model ships on display.
Haigh Terrace, Dun Laoghaire. Tel: 01–280 0969. Open: May to September, Tuesday to Sunday and public holidays 2.30–5.30pm. Admission charge.

NEWBRIDGE HOUSE

This Georgian house, built in 1737 for the Cobbe family, is now owned by Dublin County Council. A wealth of paintings hangs in the drawing room, and cabinets display all manner of antique curiosities brought back by the Cobbe family from their extensive world travels. The cobbled square has been restored and recently opened as a farm and museum of 18th-century rural life. There is also an aviary and a doll museum.

Donabate. Tel: 01–843 6534/5. Open: April to October, Tuesday to Friday 10am–1pm, 2–5pm, Saturday 11am–6pm, Sunday and public holidays 2–6pm; November to March, Saturday, Sunday and public holidays 2–5pm. Admission charge.

CO LOUTH
BATTLE OF THE BOYNE SITE
At the county borders of Louth and Meath, a large orange and green sign marks the site where the armies of William of Orange and James II met in battle in 1690. The places where each side camped and where the river was crossed are also marked. A trail leaflet is available at the site.
7km west of Drogheda. Freely accessible.

MELLIFONT ABBEY
Little remains of Ireland's first Cistercian monastery, founded in 1142, though a substantial square gatehouse still stands, along with the ruins of a cloister, a two-storey octagonal lavabo and a 13th-century chapter house.
10km west of Drogheda, signposted on unclassified roads. Freely accessible.

MILLMOUNT MUSEUM
The buildings of an 18th-century military barracks now contain centuries-old relics of Drogheda's past, including painted banners of the old trade guilds, household and factory artefacts, and a leather-covered circular coracle.
Drogheda. Tel: 041–36391. Open: May to October, daily 3–6pm; November to April, Wednesday and Sunday 3–6pm. Free.

PROLEEK DOLMEN
This 5,000-year-old massive mushroom-like stone structure has a capstone weighing over 46 tonnes. A Bronze Age wedge-shaped gallery grave is located near by.
Ballymascanlon, 7km northeast of Dundalk. Freely accessible.

Twelfth-century Malahide Castle

CO MEATH
BOYNE VALLEY
ARCHAEOLOGICAL PARK

The Boyne Valley Archaeological Site encompasses over 40 monuments, ranging from the massive megalithic tombs of Newgrange, Knowth and Dowth to a variety of standing stones and earthworks. Newgrange, one of Europe's most important Stone Age sites, is open to the public, but there are often queues for guided tours. The Newgrange passage grave, over 4,000 years old and predating the Pyramids of Egypt, is an extraordinary sight. The mound over the tomb, constructed of water-rolled pebbles, rises to a height of 11m, and is surrounded by an incomplete circle of stones. The passage is lined with huge stones, and mysterious 'artwork' in the form of geometrical symbols and spirals can be seen inside. A roof box incorporated in the structure allows the rays of the rising sun to penetrate a narrow slit and engulf the chamber with light – just briefly, once a year at the winter solstice. This phenomenon is reproduced artificially for the benefit of visitors. An interpretative centre and shop are on the site. *11km southwest of Drogheda. Tel: 041–24488. Open: June to mid-September, daily 10am–7pm; mid-March to May and mid-September to October, daily 10am–1pm, 2–5pm; November to mid-March, Tuesday to Sunday 10am–1pm, 2–4.30pm. Admission charge.*

HILL OF TARA

Famous as the seat of the High Kings of Ireland and an important site since the Stone Age, when a passage tomb was built, this was a major political and religious centre in early Christian times. Commanding majestic views over the fertile plains of Meath, it was abandoned in AD1022 and now consists of grass-covered mounds, banks, wide ditches and earthworks. Inside the Mound of Hostages, a passage grave dated some 2,000 years BC, the skeleton of a boy wearing a necklace of bronze, amber and jet was found.
Tara, 13km south of Navan. Tel: 046–25903. Open: year-round, daily. Telephone to check times of guided tours, if required. Freely accessible.

KELLS

Monks from Iona in Scotland took refuge in a monastery here after being evicted by the Danes. They devoted their time to writing the *Book of Kells*, which was removed to the safety of Trinity College during the Cromwellian wars, and is still there (see page 41). A copy can be seen at the Church of Ireland (St Columba's) in Kells.
Kells, 16km northwest of Navan.

St Columba's churchyard, Kells

No longer producing its famous whiskey, Locke's Distillery is now a museum

NEWGRANGE
See Boyne Valley Archaeological Park (opposite).

SLANE HILL
It was here in 433, tradition has it, that St Patrick proclaimed the arrival of Christianity. The hill provides a splendid view of the Boyne Valley in fine weather.
13km west of Drogheda.

CO WESTMEATH
ATHLONE CASTLE
The Anglo-Norman castle was a military post from its erection in the 13th century until 1969, when it was declared a National Monument controlled by the Office of Public Works. The visitor centre, with its museum and visual display, opened in 1991 to mark the tercentenary of the Siege of Athlone. There is a military museum in the keep, with relics of the town and district's history.
Athlone, on west bank of the River Shannon. Tel: 0902–94603. Open: 1 April to 21 October, Monday to Saturday 10am–6pm, Sunday noon–6pm. By arrangement from November to March. Admission charge.

LOCKE'S DISTILLERY
Founded in 1757 and operational until 1953, this distillery, on the River Brosna, has been restored as an industrial museum and craft enterprise centre with a café.
Kilbeggan, on the Dublin to Galway road (N6). Tel: 0506–32134. Open: April to October, daily 9am–6pm; November to March, daily 10am–4pm. Admission charge.

Ireland's is a landscape of fantasy. Every scene, it seems – on mountainside, river bank or rocky shore – bears an exclamation mark of history in the form of a round tower or ruined castle.

Close your eyes and it is not difficult to conjure up figures from the past: hooded monks sprinting across the turf and pulling up the ladders against another gang of Viking raiders; minstrels making music while the lords and ladies feast; silhouettes flitting among flames as dark deeds are committed.

TOWERS

The 70 or so pencil-shaped round towers – unique to Ireland – which survive throughout the country date mainly from the ninth century. Built near ecclesiastical sites, especially monasteries, they served as belltowers, storehouses and watch-towers.

Varying in height from 15 to 45m, and usually tapering towards a stone cone-shaped top, the towers had a door set high enough above the ground to require a ladder for entry. This could be hauled in during an attack. Most towers originally had a number of floors reached by ladders and trapdoors, but some, probably used only as watch-towers, had a stairway. Among the best-preserved towers are those at Ardmore, Co Waterford; Cashel, Co Tipperary; Cloyne, Co Cork; Devenish Island, Co Fermanagh; Glendalough, Co Wicklow; and Monasterboice, Co Louth.

TOWERS AND CASTLES

The first stone castles – the earliest were timber constructions – were built by Norman colonists between 1190 and 1215. The grandest were those in Dublin, Kilkenny and Limerick.

Many of Ireland's castles date from a 15th-century building boom among such influential families as the MacCarthys (Blarney, Co Cork), the MacConmaras (Bunratty, Co Clare) and the MacNamaras (Knappogue, Co Clare). Bunratty and Knappogue are best known now for hosting medieval banquets.

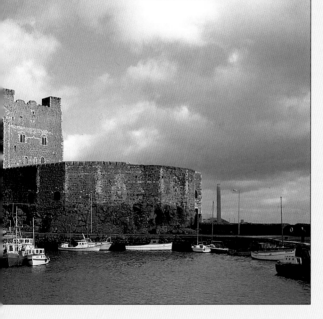

Above left: Kildare Cathedral's 10th-century round tower
Above: Kilkenny Castle, a blend of Gothic and classical styles

Left: Carrickfergus Castle was built on its rocky promontory by John de Courcy in the late 12th century

CO LONGFORD
CARRIGGLAS MANOR

Built in 1857, this fine Victorian country house, the home of the Lefroy family, contains a costume collection, as well as original furnishings. The stables were designed by James Gandon, who was also responsible for the magnificent Custom House in Dublin.

8km from Longford, on the N55. Tel: 043–45165. Open: mid-June to mid-September, Thursday to Saturday 12.30–5pm, Sunday 2.30–6pm. Admission charge.

CO OFFALY
BIRR CASTLE

Home of the Earls of Rosse, the castle is not open to the public, but the beautiful 40-hectare gardens are. Plants from remote parts of the world grow in these gardens, famous for the world's highest box hedge (10m), and for the permanent exhibition of the Rosse telescope, the world's largest when it was built in the mid-19th century.

Birr, South Offaly. Tel: 0509–20056. Open: daily 9am–1pm, 2–6pm (dusk if earlier). Admission charge.

Birr Castle, an impressive fortified manor house set in extensive grounds

BOG TOUR

Organised by Bord Na Móna (the Irish Peat Board), this is an 8km tour of the Blackwater Bog aboard a train from the Clonmacnois and West Offaly Railway. Visitors can learn of the 12,000-year development of the bog from glacier to lake, to fen and to bog.

Blackwater Works, Shannonbridge. Tel: 0905–74114. Open: April to October, Monday to Saturday 10am–5pm (tours on the hour), Sunday noon–5pm. Other times of the year by arrangement. Admission charge.

CLONMACNOIS

One of Ireland's most sacred sites, and former burial place of the kings of Connacht and Tara, this monastic settlement, founded by St Ciaran in AD545, contains two round towers, the remains of a cathedral, church ruins, high crosses, a 13th-century castle and over 200 grave slabs. The Nuns' Chapel and the 10th-century Cross of the Scriptures are particularly noted for the quality of the mason's craft. *Shannonbridge. Tel: 0905–74195. Open: mid-June to September, daily 9am–7pm; October to May, daily 10am–6pm. Admission charge.*

CO KILDARE
CASTLETOWN HOUSE

Ireland's first, and most important, Palladian mansion was built in the 1720s by William Conolly. Its elegant interior includes fine examples of 18th-century furniture and superb plaster-work by the Francini brothers. *Celbridge. Tel: 01–628 8252. Open: April to October, Monday to Friday 10am–6pm, Saturday 11am–6pm, Sunday and public holidays 2–6pm; November to March, weekends and public holidays 2–5pm. Admission charge.*

JAPANESE GARDENS

These superb gardens at the Irish National Stud were designed in 1906 for Lord Wavertree. Considered by many to be the finest in Europe, their design symbolically portrays the life of Man from the cradle to the grave. *Tully. 1.5km south of Kildare town. Tel: 045–21617. Open: Easter Sunday to October, Monday to Saturday 10.30am–5pm, Sunday 2–6pm. Admission charge.*

STEAM MUSEUM

The model railway collection here depicts the development of the Irish locomotive since the 18th century. Also on display are full-size stationary locos working under steam. *Lodge Park, Straffan. Tel: 01–627 3155. Open: mid-June to end August, daily 11.30am–5.30pm (last admission 4.30pm); Sunday and public holidays year round. Closed: Christmas to New Year. Admission charge.*

The Japanese Gardens, laid out by Japanese gardener Eida, and his son Minoru

CO LAOIS
EMO COURT AND GARDENS

Possibly the premier attraction in the county, this fine Georgian mansion was designed by James Gandon, architect of Dublin's Custom House. Its great rotunda is lit by a lantern in the dome. The gardens contain fine statuary, rare trees, an imposing lake, shrubs and avenues of yews.

Emo. Tel: 0502–26110. House open: mid-June to mid-September, daily 2–6pm; gardens, daily 10.30am–5.30pm. Admission charge.

STEAM AND VINTAGE MACHINERY MUSEUM

Steam road engines and rollers operate here during traction engine rallies and railway events, with rides on Irish Peat Board loco-hauled coaches on narrow gauge railway, while displays portray the progress of steam in Ireland.

Irish Steam Preservation Society, The Green, Stradbally. Tel: 0502–25444. Open: for rallies. Admission charge.

WINDY GAP

The Carlow to Stradbally road (N8) passes through Windy Gap, one of Ireland's most famous scenic drives. Stop at the Windy Gap car park for a long look over the Barrow Valley, with its wide vistas of the surrounding countryside.

CO CARLOW
ALTAMOUNT GARDENS

These fine gardens were planted in 1850, with a lily pool, arboretum, and a bog garden.

Off the N81 between Tullow and Bunclody. Tel: 0503–59128. Open: Easter Sunday and every Sunday and public holiday to the end of October, 2–6pm. Admission charge.

Ruins at the tiny hamlet of Avoca

BROWNE'S HILL DOLMEN

This impressive dolmen, dating from around 2000BC, has the largest capstone in Ireland, estimated to weigh more than 101 tonnes. The front end is supported by three uprights, while the rear has collapsed and rests on the ground.
On the R725, about 3km northeast of Carlow town towards Tullow. Freely accessible.

CARLOW CASTLE

Carlow's ruined 13th-century castle has witnessed much bloodshed in its turbulent history. It survived Cromwell's forces in the 17th century, but was badly damaged 150 years later during attempts to reduce the thickness of the walls with explosives. The castle is on private property near the east bank of the River Barrow in Carlow town, but permission to look more closely may be obtained from the adjacent Corcoran's Mineral Water factory.

CO WICKLOW

AVOCA

The little village of Avoca is set in its picturesque valley, where the confluence of two rivers, the Avonbeg and the Avonmore inspired Thomas Moore to write his famous poem *The Meeting of the Waters* in 1807. The oldest hand-weaving mill in Ireland, Avoca Hand-weavers, still produces textiles in the traditional way and welcomes visitors.
4km south of Avondale. Handweavers – tel: 0402–35105. Open: Monday to Friday 9.30am–5.30pm; weekends 10am–5.30pm. Free.

AVONDALE HOUSE

Avondale is the restored home of the nationalist leader, Charles Stewart Parnell (1846–91). Part of the house is devoted to a museum.
Rathdrum. Tel: 0404–46111. Open: Easter to end September, Monday to Saturday 11am–6pm, Sunday 1–6pm. Admission charge for house.

GLENDALOUGH

Glendalough is the setting of Ireland's most important early Christian settlement, founded by St Kevin in the 6th century. It grew into a centre of learning and its fame spread throughout Europe. Among the ruins are a near-perfect round tower, a church with fine Irish Romanesque decoration, an oratory (St Kevin's Kitchen) and a 10th-century cathedral. An interpretative centre is run at the site by the Office of Public Works.
16km west of Wicklow. Tel: 0404–45351/2. Open: daily from 10am (closed Monday from November to mid-March). Closing times vary from 4.30pm in winter to 7pm mid-June to mid-September. Admission charge.

MOUNT USHER GARDENS

Mount Usher is one of the finest examples of a 'wild garden', planted along the banks of the River Vartry. Laid out in 1868, it contains rare trees, shrubs and flowers from all over the world, including 70 species of eucalyptus.
Ashford, on the main Dublin/Wicklow road. Tel: 0404–40116. Open: mid-March to end October, Monday to Saturday 10.30am–6pm, Sunday 11am–6pm. Admission charge.

The gardens at Mount Usher are set along the banks of its winding stream

POWERSCOURT GARDENS

The main block of this Palladian-style house was gutted by fire in 1974. But the gardens, among the finest in Europe, live on. They include English, Italian and Japanese sections and are rich in sculptures, a fountain and terraces, formal flower beds and tall conifers. Some 5km away is spectacular Powerscourt Waterfall, at 120m the highest in Ireland.

Enniskerry, near Bray. Tel: 01–286 7676. Open: March to October, daily 9am– 5.30pm; waterfall all year. Admission charge.

Powerscourt, one of Ireland's great gardens, uses ornamental features to good effect

RUSSBOROUGH HOUSE

This mid-18th-century mansion with its sumptuous plasterwork is home to the Beit Art Collection, which includes works by Gainsborough, Murillo and Velázquez. The rhododendron garden is open in late spring.

Blessington. Tel: 045–65239. Open: Easter to end October, Sunday and public holidays 10.30am–5.30pm; June to August, daily 10.30am–5.30pm. Admission charge.

CO KILKENNY

CITYSCOPE EXHIBITION

Housed in the 16th-century Shee Alms House, Cityscope is a three-dimensional scale model of 17th-century Kilkenny City, with other small-scale exhibits.

Rose Inn Street, Kilkenny. Tel: 056– 51500. Open: March to September, daily 9am–5pm; October and November, Monday to Friday 9am–5pm. Admission charge.

DUNMORE CAVE

Human bones and coins found in this natural limestone cavern suggest that Vikings caused the deaths of many people, including children, in 928. Well-lit walkways lead past enormous stalagmite and stalactite formations, and a small centre explains the history and geology of the cave system.

11km north of Kilkenny, on the N78. Tel: 056–67726. Open: mid-March to mid-June, Tuesday to Saturday 10am–5pm, Sunday 2–5pm; mid-June to mid-September, daily 10am–5pm; winter, weekends and public holidays 10am–5pm. Admission charge.

JERPOINT ABBEY

This 12th-century Cistercian abbey is one of Ireland's finest monastic ruins. Its extensive remains are awe-inspiring, and it has particularly fine, detailed carvings in the cloisters.

1.5km south of Thomastown, on the N9. Tel: 056–24623. Open: April to mid-June, Tuesday to Sunday 10am–1pm, 2–5pm; mid-June to September, daily 9.30am– 6.30pm; early October, daily 10am–1pm, 2–5pm. Admission charge.

KILKENNY CASTLE

Set above the waters of the River Nore, imposing 12th-century Kilkenny Castle is noted for its restored great hall and

tapestries. Opposite, in the stables, is the prestigious Kilkenny Design Centre.
Kilkenny. Tel: 056–21450. Open: April and May, daily 10.30am–5pm; June to September, daily 10am–7pm; October to March, Tuesday to Saturday 10.30am– 12.45pm, 2–5pm, Sunday 11am– 12.45pm, 2–5pm. Admission charge.

KILKENNY CATHEDRAL
Renowned for its grandeur, carvings and marble monuments, St Canice's Cathedral was built in the 13th century. The neighbouring round tower dates from the 6th century.
Dean Street, Kilkenny. Tel: 056–64971. Open: Monday to Saturday 9am–1pm, 2–6pm (10am–1pm, 2–4pm October to April), Sunday 2–6pm. Admission charge for round tower.

CO WEXFORD
IRISH NATIONAL HERITAGE PARK
This excellent, open-air site is a good introduction to Ireland, from prehistoric to medieval times, including authentic reconstructions of Stone Age and Bronze Age fortifications and settlements and a Norman motte and bailey.
Ferrycarrig. Tel: 053–20733. Open: March to October, daily 10am–7pm (last admission 5pm). Admission charge.

JOHN F KENNEDY PARK AND ARBORETUM
Situated above the Kennedy ancestral home, this collection of 4,500 types of trees and shrubs is set in 252 hectares. In summer, visitors can tour it by pony and trap or miniature railway.
Dunganstown, New Ross. Tel: 051–388171. Open: daily from 10am (closing time varies according to time of year). Admission charge.

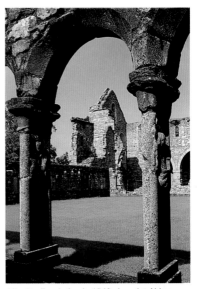

After its dissolution in 1540, Jerpoint Abbey was granted to the Ormonde family

WEXFORD MEDIEVAL EXPERIENCE
An audio-visual presentation of the town's early history is appropriately set in an early 13th-century gate tower, part of the town's Viking/Norman walls.
Westgate Heritage Centre, Wexford. Tel: 053–46506. Open: March to December, Monday to Saturday 10am–2pm, 2.30–5.30pm (also July and August, Sunday 2–6pm). Admission charge.

WEXFORD WILDFOWL RESERVE
Bewick swans, white-fronted geese, pintails, gulls and other species winter on the mudflats of this wildlife reserve on the Slaney Estuary. There are walks, an observation tower and charts to assist visitors with identification.
North Sloblands. Tel: 053–23129. Open: all year. Freely accessible.

Dublin's Old City

This area has witnessed the Dublin story from its very beginnings. Here, the Vikings settled in 841. Some 300 years later, Strongbow stormed the city, and a castle was built. *Allow 1½ hours.*

Begin on Wellington Quay with Ha'penny Bridge behind you and head south.

1 TEMPLE BAR AREA
This maze of narrow streets has developed into an arty area of bistros, boutiques and art galleries, all tucked into the ageing warehouses formally occupied by merchants and craftsmen.
Head west (right) along Temple Bar, then turn left into Temple Lane and continue to Dame Street.

2 DAME STREET
Dame Street once provided access to the nunnery of St Mary del Dame, but its name derives from a dam once built on the River Poddle, now running underground. Dublin's oldest surviving theatre, the Olympia, was opened here in 1870.
Turn left into Castle Street. Ahead is the gate to Upper Castle Yard.

Nearby

4 Marsh's Library
(see page 31)

3 DUBLIN CASTLE
Work on the castle began in 1205, although there are indications that defensive earthworks existed before the Vikings arrived. Guided tours of the castle and state apartments are normally available (see page 26).
Leave by the Justice Gate. Continue left along Castle Street; turn left into Werburgh and Bride streets. After turning right into Kevin Street Upper, turn right again into St Patrick's Close.

4 ST PATRICK'S CATHEDRAL
Standing on a site traditionally associated with Ireland's patron saint, St Patrick's Cathedral was dedicated in 1192. A bust of Jonathan Swift, author of _Gulliver's Travels_, is at the west end of the nave (see page 39).
Turn right into Patrick Street, left into Back Lane and right into High Street.

5 HIGH STREET
The Tailor's Hall in Back Lane, built around 1706, is Dublin's last surviving Guild Hall. The 'Back Lane Parliament' met here in 1792. St Audoen's, the city's oldest surviving medieval parish church, has a 12th-century tower, 15th-century nave and a font dating from 1194. The 'Flame on the Hill' audio-visual presentation in neighbouring St Audoen's Roman Catholic Church, tells the story of life in pre-Viking Ireland (see page 38).
Cross Nicholas Street/Winetavern Street to Christ Church Place.

6 CHRIST CHURCH PLACE
Built in the mid-11th century and re-built in stone by the Anglo-Normans, Christ Church Cathedral contains the tomb of Strongbow, Earl of Pembroke (see page 24).

Twelfth-century Christ Church Cathedral replaced a timber-built church

Bear left along Christ Church Place to Fishamble Street.

7 FISHAMBLE STREET
This was the home of Dublin's fish market before becoming fashionable. It was the birthplace of Archbishop Ussher, the poet James Clarence Mangan and the nationalist Henry Grattan, and witnessed the first performance of Handel's _Messiah_.
At the river turn right into Essex Quay.

8 ESSEX QUAY
At the western end of Essex Quay, the Franciscan church of SS Michael and John incorporates the remains of the Smock-Alley Theatre, built in 1661 and closed in the 1790s when the gallery collapsed during a performance. At the eastern end, Sunlight Chambers, built around 1900, has an ornate terracotta frieze illustrating the manufacture and uses of soap.
Cross Parliament Street and continue along Wellington Quay to end the walk back at Ha'penny Bridge.

Dublin's Cultural Heart

Dublin north of the Liffey is the city's cultural heart. Here are the widest and largest streets, the best Georgian houses and the most splendid public buildings. Here also are the Abbey and Gate theatres. *Allow 2 hours.*

Begin on the north side of O'Connell Bridge, following Eden Quay to Custom House Quay.

1 CUSTOM HOUSE

Dublin's most magnificent building, Custom House was designed by James Gandon. Since its opening in 1792, it has survived three major fires – the last, in 1921, was so fierce that brass fittings melted (see page 26).
Return to Butt Bridge, then turn right into Beresford Place.

Nearby

4 Hugh Lane Municipal Gallery of Modern Art

2 ABBEY STREET

The Abbey Theatre, on the corner of Marlborough Street, was founded in 1904 by a group led by W B Yeats (see page 24).

Opposite are the offices of the National Lottery, instituted to provide funds for the arts, culture and sport.
Turn right into O'Connell Street.

3 O'CONNELL STREET

O'Connell Street is one of the world's great thoroughfares. It is dominated by the Georgian majesty of the General Post Office, which was shelled and set ablaze when it became headquarters of the Irish Volunteers in the Easter Rising of 1916 (see page 27). O'Connell Street has many associations with Ireland's struggle for independence.

The statue of a gigantic maiden lying in the running waters of a stream, in the central mall, is the Anna Livia Millennium Fountain, symbolising the spirit of the Liffey – Dubliners call it 'the Floozie in the Jacuzzi'.
Cross Parnell Street to Parnell Square East.

4 PARNELL SQUARE

Originally known as the Barley Fields, Parnell Square dates from 1748 when it was laid out as pleasure gardens. On the left, beyond the monument to Charles Stewart Parnell, is the Gate Theatre, built in 1786 and converted to a theatre in 1930. Parnell Square North houses the Dublin Writers' Museum (see pages 26–7).
Turn right into Granby Row.

5 GRANBY ROW

Granby Row was the work of the Georgian developer Luke Gardiner, who had a profound influence throughout the city. The National Wax Museum is on the corner with Dorset Street (see page 33).
Turn left into Dorset Street. Continue along Bolton Street and turn right into Henrietta Street.

6 HENRIETTA STREET

Another Gardiner development, this was once the most fashionable street in Dublin, housing at one time in the mid-18th century five peers, a peeress, a peer's son, a judge, a Member of Parliament, a bishop and two wealthy clergymen.
At the end of Henrietta Street pass through the central arch of King's Inns and cross the park to Constitution Hill. Turning left, continue to Church Street. Turn right into May Lane.

7 IRISH WHISKEY CORNER

Visitors get the chance to taste the different blends of Irish whiskey in this museum for adults, set in a former bonded warehouse in Jameson's old distillery (see page 30).
Turn left on to Bow Street and left again along Hammond Lane to Church Street.

8 ST MICHAN'S CHURCH

St Michan's contains a magnificent organ on which Handel is believed to have played. It also has a Penitent's Stool and a 16th-century chalice. But the church is best known for its limestone vaults where mummified bodies are on view (see page 38).
Head south along Church Street, turning left on to Inns Quay.

9 FOUR COURTS

Designed by Gandon and completed in 1802, the massive Georgian edifice confronting the Liffey is the seat of the Irish Law Courts. Columns of the portico still bear battle scars inflicted in 1922 when the building was shelled during the civil war (see page 27).
Continue parallel to the Liffey along Ormond Quay and complete the walk back at O'Connell Bridge.

Munster

*A*s well as Co Tipperary, Ireland's largest inland county, Munster contains the counties of Waterford, Cork, Kerry, Limerick and Clare. Its terrain is as varied as Ireland itself, from the Golden Plain of Tipperary to the rugged coastlines of Cork, the mountains of Kerry and the majestic Cliffs of Moher in Clare. Here, the past and present merge. The ancient ringforts and dolmens and the mystic Rock of Cashel share the province with three of Ireland's largest industrial cities: Cork, Limerick and Waterford.

CO TIPPERARY
BRU BORU HERITAGE CENTRE
Named after Brian Ború, the 11th-century High King of Ireland, this cultural village incorporates a folk theatre, craft centre, information centre and a computerised genealogy service. Banquets, music and drama are nightly events in summer, and the restaurant serves Irish fare.

Cashel's excellent folk village portrays rural life

Adjoining the Rock of Cashel. Tel: 062–61122. Open: April to September, daily 9am–11pm; October to March, Monday to Friday 9am–5pm. Free.

CAHIR CASTLE
Built on a rocky island in the middle of the River Suir, Cahir Castle, one of the best preserved in Ireland, has been impressively restored. Built in the 15th and 16th centuries, its oldest parts date from 1164. Furnishings are authentic reproductions of the period. Scenes for the films *Excalibur* and *Barry Lyndon* were shot here, and there are guided tours. An audio-visual presentation highlights the area's antiquities.
Cahir. Tel: 052–641011. Open: April to mid-June and mid-September to mid-October, daily 10am–6pm; mid-June to mid-September, daily 9am–7.30pm; mid-October to March, daily 10am–1pm, 2–4.30pm. Admission charge.

CASHEL FOLK VILLAGE
Cashel's Folk Village is an interesting collection of reconstructed houses and shops displaying furniture, artefacts and tools portraying local life from the 18th to 20th centuries.
Main Street, Cashel. Tel: 062–62525. Open: March and April, daily 10am–6pm; May to October, daily 9.30am–7.30pm. Admission charge.

MUNSTER

Galway
Galway Bay
N6 Ballinasloe
Grand Canal
Tullamore
Aran
Islands
N18 Loughrea
Shannon
Birr
Slieve Bloom Mts
N7
Aillwee
Cave Gort
The
Burren
Lahinch
Hags Head
Ennistymon
Lough
Derg
Roscrea
Portlaoise
Dublin
Ennis Craggaunowen
N18 Project
Bunratty
Nenagh
N7
Durrow
Carlow
Kilkee
Kilrush
Foynes
LIMERICK
Suir
Thurles
Loop Head Tarbert
Ballybunion
Newcastle
West
Patrickswell N24
Lough Gur
Holycross
Bru
Boru
Kilkenny
N9
Callan
N10
Kerry Head Listowel
Tipperary
Cashel
Fethard
Abbeyfeale
Galtee Mts
Clonmel Carrick-
on-Suir
Gallarus
Oratory 953m
Tralee N21
Donerail Mitchelstown Caves
Cahir
755m
WATERFORD
Dunquin Dingle Castlegregory
Forest Park
Knockmealdown Mts
Kilbarry
Blasket Is Fahan
Dingle Bay
Lough
Leane
Killarney
Blackwater
Mallow
Lismore Lemybrien N25
Tramore
Valentia
Island Cahirciveen
1041m
Muckross
Kenmare
Boggeragh
Mts
Macroom
Blarney
Castle
N20 N8
Midleton
Youghal
Ardmore
Dungarvan
Dunmore
East
Derrynane
House
Gougane Barra
Forest Park
Lee
CORK
Youghal
Bay
Skellig
Rock
Kenmare River
Glengarriff 695m
Bantry
Dunmanway
Cobh
Cloyne
Roches
Pt
Dursey
Island
Bantry Bay
Clonakilty
Skibbereen
Timoleague
Kinsale
Old Head
of Kinsale
Schull
Ross
Carbery
Mizen
Head
C Clear
Baltimore

0 20 40km
0 20mls

CASHEL HERITAGE CENTRE

The story of the Kings of Cashel from AD300 is featured in Cashel's Heritage Centre.
Main Street, Cashel. Tel: 062–61846. Open: daily 9am–6pm. Admission charge.

FETHARD FOLK, FARM AND TRANSPORT MUSEUM

More than 2,500 items arranged in a series of 'real-life' reconstructions are displayed in the freight depot of an old railway station. Major features include a forge, a country kitchen, a jaunting car, a baker's van and a horse-drawn hearse.

Cashel Road, Fethard. Tel: 052–31516. Open: June to August, daily 10.30am–5pm; September to May, Sunday 1–5pm. Admission charge.

GPA BOLTON LIBRARY

This library has a fine collection of illuminated manuscripts, books and maps. Exhibitions of printing, antique books and silver are frequently staged.
Grounds of St John the Baptist Cathedral, John Street, Cashel. Tel: 062–61232/ 71332. Open: March to November, Monday to Saturday 9.30am–5pm, Sunday 2.30–5.30pm. Admission charge.

HOLY CROSS ABBEY

Founded in 1180, left derelict for 400 years and restored totally between 1971 and 1985, the abbey thrives as a parish church. It incorporates architecture of the 12th and 15th centuries, with excellent stone carvings and window traceries.
Holycross, 6km south of Thurles, on the R660. Tel: 0504–43241. Open: all times. Donation appreciated.

Detail of stone carving at the Rock of Cashel

MITCHELSTOWN CAVE

Visitors can take an escorted tour through the spectacular rock formations of these massive, high-ceilinged chambers, only discovered in recent times.
Burncourt, midway between Cahir and Mitchelstown. Tel: 052–67246. Open: Monday to Friday 10am–5pm, weekends 2.30–5pm. Admission charge.

NENAGH HERITAGE CENTRE

Nenagh's former county gaol houses the town's Heritage Centre. It features the excellent Lifestyles in Northwest Tipperary Exhibition and there are frequent temporary displays of paintings and photographs.
Opposite the Castle Keep, Nenagh. Tel: 067–32633. Open: mid-May to end

October, Monday to Friday 10am–5pm, weekends 2.30–5pm. Admission charge.

ORMONDE CASTLE

Ireland's best example of a fortified Elizabethan manor house, Ormonde Castle was built in 1584 alongside an older building overlooking the River Suir. It is said to have been built by the Earl of Ormonde, to entertain Queen Elizabeth I, who never arrived. The older castle is said to be the birthplace of Anne Boleyn, wife of Henry VIII.
Carrick-on-Suir. Tel: 051–640787. Open: mid-June to September, daily 9.30am–6.30pm. Admission charge.

ROCK OF CASHEL

The Rock of Cashel – the Gaelic word means 'stone fort' – soars 60m above the Golden Vale. Legend has it that the Devil took a bite out of the nearby Slieve Bloom Mountains and spat it out on to the plains when he was surprised by St Patrick.

Crowning the rock is a wealth of medieval architecture. The oldest building, the Round Tower, is thought to date from the 10th century, but it is certain that the site was hallowed in pre-Christian times. The High Kings of Munster are said to have been crowned on the summit.

Cormac's Chapel, completed in 1134, is the best-preserved of the Rock's buildings and is also the earliest of Ireland's surviving Romanesque churches. It was built by Cormac Macarthy, King of Desmond and Bishop of Cashel, and its twisted columns, steeply-pitched roof and fantastic carvings contribute to its unique beauty.

St Patrick's Cathedral, the largest building, was built about a century later than the chapel. The 13th-century building was burned down in 1495 and restored in the 16th century. The Apostles and scenes from the Apocalypse are represented in sculptures in the north transept, and there is a splendid view of the surrounding vale from the top of the central tower.

The Hall of Vicars is the first building to be reached by those approaching the Rock from Cashel town. It was built in the 15th century for eight vicars who assisted in the cathedral services. On the ground floor is the original St Patrick's Cross (the one outside is a replica), a high cross less ornately carved than usual.
Cashel. Tel: 062–61437. Open: mid-March to mid-June, daily 9.30am–5.30pm; mid-June to mid-September, daily 9am–7pm; mid-September to mid-March, daily 9.30am–4.30pm. (Last admission 45 minutes before closing.) Admission charge.

TIPPERARY COUNTY MUSEUM
This permanent display of 19th- and early 20th-century items of political, civic and industrial interest also has frequent exhibitions staged in association with the National Museum and Library.
Municipal Library, Parnell Street, Clonmel. Tel: 052–25399. Open: Tuesday to Saturday 10am–1pm, 2–5pm. Free.

Rock of Cashel, stronghold of the kings of Munster for over 700 years

Christ Church Cathedral, Waterford, built to
the same plan as Dublin's Christ Church

CO WATERFORD
ARDMORE MONASTIC SITE

According to legend, 30 years before St
Patrick arrived in Ireland in the 5th
century, St Declan crossed from Wales
and established a monastic settlement at
Ardmore. He chose a magnificent
location, affording stunning views over
the bay, and as a result of his arrival the
area surrounding the site is known to
this day as Old Parish – believed to be
the oldest parish in Ireland.

The site of the saint's original
monastic foundation is today marked by
an exceptionally well-preserved 11th-
century round tower in the ruined
Cathedral of St Declan. The
surrounding graveyard, pitching steeply
towards the coast, contains St Declan's

Oratory, where the saint is believed to
be buried. Roofless though it is, the
old cathedral is an evocative place,
especially when one views the strikingly
carved murals depicting the *Adoration of
the Magi*, the *Fall of Man*, the *Judgement
of Solomon* and the *Weighing of Souls*.
*Signposted off the N25 between Dungarvan,
(Co Waterford) and Youghal (Co Cork).
Freely accessible.*

CELTWORLD

The mystery and mythology of Celtic
life in early Ireland is told in a high-tech
presentation which employs three-
dimensional images and larger-than-life
moving figures.
*Widely indicated in Tramore. Tel: 051–
86166. Open: June to September, daily
10am–11pm; March to May and October,
daily 10am–5.30pm; November to
February, weekends and pre-booked parties.
Admission charge.*

CHRIST CHURCH CATHEDRAL

Designed by John Roberts, a Waterford
architect whose work included the city's
Holy Trinity Cathedral, Christ Church
is an ornate Renaissance-style structure
built in the 1770s to replace a church
which had stood on the site since the
11th century. Standing in a pleasant
square, the Church of Ireland cathedral
contains interesting monuments,
including the 15th-century tomb of
James Rice, depicting a decaying corpse.

Across the square from the cathedral
is the roofless French Church, founded
as a Franciscan friary in 1240 and later
used by Huguenot refugees. It has a fine
east window and the tomb of Sir Neal
O'Neill, who fled with James II after the
Battle of the Boyne.
*Cathedral Square, Waterford. Freely
accessible.*

HOLY TRINITY CATHEDRAL

The simple exterior of Waterford's Roman Catholic cathedral, also designed by John Roberts, conceals an extravagantly decorated interior hung with chandeliers of Waterford crystal.
Barronstrand Street, Waterford. Freely accessible.

LEMYBRIEN DOLL EXHIBITION

This private collector's display has antique dolls and toys dating from 1820.
On the N25 in Lemybrien, 10km northeast of Dungarvan. Tel: 051–91147. Open: 1 June to 1 September, Monday to Saturday 2–9pm, Sunday 4–9pm. Admission charge.

LISMORE CASTLE GARDENS

One of several places linked with Edmund Spenser's poem *The Faerie Queene*, the gardens have a fine collection of shrubs, including camellias and magnolias, and restful woodland walks. A dramatic yew walk is believed to be more than 800 years old. The Irish home of the Dukes of Devonshire, the estate was once leased to Sir Walter Raleigh.

The present castle, built in the mid-19th century, is not open to the public.
Signposted in Lismore. Tel: 058–54424. Open: Garden tours – May to September, Sunday to Friday 1.45–4.45pm. Admission charge.

LISMORE EXPERIENCE

Lismore has a rich history: founded as a monastic centre in AD636, it became a famous seat of learning, was sacked repeatedly by Vikings and Normans, and became involved in many religious and political struggles. The story is told in this new audio-visual presentation.
Open: May to September, Monday to Friday 10am–5pm, weekends 2.30–5.30pm; October, Sunday 2.30–5.30pm. Free.

Right: Lismore Experience relates the town's long and varied history
Below: spectacularly lit Lismore Castle

REGINALD'S TOWER

Built by the Vikings in 1003 as part of Waterford's defences, the squat but massive tower has walls 3m thick and stands 25m high. In its time it has served as a royal residence, a mint, a gaol and an arsenal. It is now a civic museum.

The Mall, Waterford. Tel: 051–873501. Open: daily 10am–5pm. Admission charge.

Reginald's Tower takes its name from Ragnvald the Dane, who supposedly built it

WATERFORD CITY HALL

This fine Georgian building dates from 1783 and incorporates the Theatre Royal, where the city's Festival of Light Music is staged every October. A huge Waterford glass chandelier, made in 1802, hangs in the council chamber (a copy can be found in Philadelphia's Independence Hall). The uniform and sword of Thomas Francis Meagher, a Waterford man who fought in the Irish Brigade at Fredericksburg in the American Civil War, is included in a collection of military memorabilia.

The Mall, Waterford. Tel: 051–873501. Open: Monday to Friday 9am–1pm, 2–5pm. Free.

WATERFORD GLASS FACTORY

Self-guided tours of the famous factory must be arranged in advance. Examples of Waterford Crystal can be seen in the gallery display area afterwards.

Cork Road, Kilbarry, 1.5km from Waterford, on the N25. Tel: 051–873311. Open: April to October, daily 8.30am–6pm (tours until 4pm); November to March, Monday to Friday 9am–5pm (tours until 3.15pm). Charge for tours; gallery free.

WATERFORD HERITAGE CENTRE

Viking and Norman artefacts unearthed during extensive excavations in the city in the 1980s are displayed in a former 19th-century church. The exhibition – only a selection of some of the 75,000 items uncovered – includes leatherware, pottery and jewellery.

Greyfriars Street, Waterford. Tel: 051– 871227. Open: April, May and September, Monday to Friday 10am–1pm, 2–6pm, Saturday 10am–1pm; June to September, Monday to Friday 10am–8pm, Saturday 10am–1pm, 2–5pm. Admission charge.

CO CORK
BANTRY HOUSE

Exquisitely set in Italianate gardens overlooking the magnificent bay, this Georgian mansion dates from 1739. There are extensive collections of art and antiques, including a tapestry made for Marie-Antoinette. The French Armada Interpretive Centre, also located here, contains documents,

Intricate detail being engraved on a fine example of Waterford Crystal

weapons and artefacts from a ship which sank during the French invasion attempt of 1796.
Signposted in Bantry. Tel: 027–50047. Open: daily 9am–6pm (until 8pm in high summer). Admission charge.

BLARNEY CASTLE

Built around 1446, the castle was the stronghold of the MacCarthys, and it was Dermot MacCarthy, Lord Blarney, whose smooth talk and empty promises exasperated Elizabeth I and brought a new word into the English language. To acquire this 'gift of the gab' (eloquence), visitors must first climb over 120 steps, then lie on their back, hang over an open space and kiss the legendary Blarney Stone. The central keep, all that remains of the old castle, is set in pleasantly landscaped gardens and there are good views of the surrounding Lee Valley.
8km northwest of Cork on the R617. Tel: 021–385252. Open: May, Monday to Saturday 9am–7pm, Sunday 9.30am–5.30pm; June and July, Monday to

Saturday 9am–8.30pm, Sunday 9.30am–5.30pm; August, Monday to Saturday 9am–7.30pm, Sunday 9am–5.30pm; September, Monday to Saturday 9am–6.30pm, Sunday 9.30am–5.30pm; off-season, Sunday 9.30am–sunset. Admission charge.*

CHARLES FORT

Built in the late 17th century after the defeat of the Spanish and Irish in the Battle of Kinsale, this is one of Europe's most complete star forts (so-called because of its shape). Covering some 5 hectares on a clifftop site, it was occupied by British troops until 1920.
Summer Cove, 3km east of Kinsale. Tel: 021–772684. Open: mid-April to mid-June, Tuesday to Saturday 9am–5pm, Sunday 2–5pm; mid-June to mid-September, daily 9am–6.30pm. Admission charge.

Braving the dizzying height to kiss the legendary Blarney Stone

FLORA AND FAUNA

Ireland preserves natural habitats which have disappeared from the rest of Europe. Naturalists from all over the world visit unique locations like The Burren to see Arctic and Mediterranean plants growing side by side. They travel to rocky islands, rich wetlands and areas still farmed traditionally to observe huge concentrations of migratory birds and species that have become rare in other countries – like the corncrake and the chough.

You are never far from the countryside in Ireland. A well-marked 3km nature trail is within 3km of Belfast city centre – at Lagan Meadows, starting at the Knightsbridge Park entrance. Here you can see kingfishers, snipe, woodcocks, reed buntings and herons.

The National Trust has built several bird hides at Strangford Lough. Migrant geese, ducks, shorebirds and seabirds gather here by the thousands at different seasons (see page 103).

Rathlin Island, off the north coast, attracts serious ornithologists with its extensive sanctuary at Kebble. Huge numbers of birds sit wing to wing on cliff ledges and rock stacks, raucously shrieking – puffins, razorbills, fulmars, guillemots (see page 126).

Otters thrive all over Ireland. Native red deer, pine martens, red squirrels, grey seals, dolphins, wild goats and hares are among mammals regularly seen. There are no snakes, however – legend has it St Patrick drove them all out of Ireland.

Cape Clear, an island off Co Cork, has an observatory built by Bristol University from which rare songbird migrants are seen, as well as seabirds (see page 127).

The nutrient-poor boglands sustain many small plants – deer sedge, bog cotton, bog rosemary, bog asphodel – and insects. Sundews, butterworts and bladderworts trap insects for sustenance.

The Burren, in Co Clare, is a vast, waterless plateau of limestone hills, drawing geologists and botanists, especially in May, when countless colourful flowers appear.

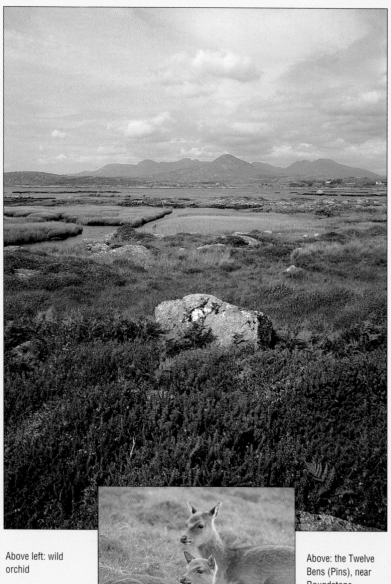

Above left: wild
orchid

Left: characteristic
Burren landscape

Above: the Twelve
Bens (Pins), near
Roundstone

Left: sika deer
at Gortin

Drombeg stone circle is one of the best preserved monuments of its kind in Ireland

DROMBEG STONE CIRCLE

The Cork-Kerry region has the highest concentration of stone circles in Ireland, and Drombeg Circle is one of the most accessible. It stands in a small field with a commanding sea view. An unusual feature of Drombeg is its communal cooking pit in which some 340 litres of water could be boiled by throwing in hot stones. A TV cook has successfully cooked a joint of meat there, using the Stone Age method.

3km west of Ross Carbery, on the R597, which loops back on to the N71 just before Leap. Freely accessible.

FOTA WILDLIFE PARK

Giraffes, kangaroos, oryx and monkeys wander freely among penguins, flamingos and peacocks, while an informal arboretum features exotic trees from all over the world. The 30-hectare park specialises in the breeding of certain endangered species.

Fota Island, Cork Harbour, 8km east of Cork on the N25. Also reached by train from Cork. Tel: 021–812678. Open: April to August, Monday to Saturday 10am–6pm, Sunday 11am–6pm; rest of year weekends only. Last admission 5.15pm. Admission charge.

GARINISH ISLAND

Rare sub-tropical plants jostle with rhododendrons, azaleas, climbing shrubs and herbaceous perennials on this colourful island in Bantry Bay, a favourite with George Bernard Shaw. The beautiful Italianate gardens, with colonnades, pools and terraces, as well as a wild garden, were laid out between 1810 and 1913.

Reached in 10 minutes by boat from Glengarriff. Tel: 027–63040. Open: March and October, Monday to Saturday 10am–4.30pm, Sunday 1–5pm; April to June and September, Monday to Saturday 10am–6.30pm, Sunday 1–6pm; July and August, Monday to Saturday 9.30am–6.30pm, Sunday 11am–6pm. Last landing one hour before closing. Admission charge.

JAMESON HERITAGE CENTRE

The story of whiskey, the mystical spirit perfected by Irish monks in the 6th century, is told in the old stone buildings of a distillery, complete with the world's largest copper still, a cast-iron mill wheel, traditional craft displays – and a generous tot at the end of the tour.

Signposted from the N25 at Midleton, 21km east of Cork. Tel: 021–613594. Open: tours – March to October, daily 10am–4.30pm. Admission charge.

MYRTLE GROVE

Sir Walter Raleigh is said to have smoked Ireland's first pipe of tobacco and planted the first potatoes at Myrtle Grove, one of the country's oldest unfortified houses, when he was Warden of Youghal in 1588–9. Edmund Spenser, the poet, also stayed at the gabled Elizabethan mansion.

Main Street, Youghal. Not accessible to the public.

Garinish's Italian gardens: George Bernard Shaw wrote much of his *St Joan* here

FAMINE AND EMIGRATION

Cobh, formerly known as Queenstown, was the embarkation point for thousands of emigrants – many of them victims of the appalling famine years of 1845–8 when Ireland's potato crop repeatedly failed as a result of blight. Facing starvation, a million people left the country for good, seeking a new life in Australia, Canada, New Zealand and the United States, and setting up huge Irish communities overseas.

ST FINN BARRE'S CATHEDRAL

The 19th-century French Gothic cathedral, with its three spires, stands on the site of a 6th-century monastery founded by St Finbarr, who also founded Cork in the early part of the 7th century (see page 77).
Bishop Street, Cork. Open: daily 9am–6pm. Free.

St Finn Barre's Cathedral, belonging to the Church of Ireland, designed by William Burges

SHANDON STEEPLE

Dominating the skyline on the north side of the River Lee in Cork, the pepperpot steeple of St Anne's Church invites visitors to entertain the entire city with music – those who climb the 37m structure can choose a tune to be played on the carillon.
Church Street, Shandon. Tel: 021–505906. Open: daily 9am–6pm. Free.

TIMOLEAGUE ABBEY AND CASTLE GARDENS

Set at the head of a long sea inlet, Timoleague Abbey was founded in 1240 and is one of Ireland's best-preserved early Franciscan friaries. Among the country's largest and most important religious houses, the monks here once traded as importers of Spanish wine.

Overlooking the abbey, palm trees and other exotic trees and shrubs flourish in beautiful walled gardens which embrace the scant ruins of 13th-century Timoleague Castle.
Signposted in the village of Timoleague. Abbey – freely accessible. Castle gardens – tel: 023–46116. Open: Easter weekend and mid-May to mid-September, daily noon– 6pm. Admission charge.

The greystone ruins of Timoleague Abbey, once Ireland's largest friary

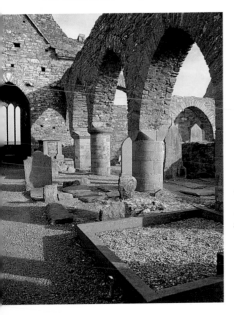

CO KERRY
DERRYNANE HOUSE AND NATIONAL HISTORIC PARK

The home of Daniel O'Connell, the 'Liberator', is now kept as a museum and memorial to the great 19th-century politician. The National Historic Park surrounding the house covers 120 hectares of sub-tropical plants, shrubs and coastal trees. There is also a nature trail, and visitors can bathe in the sea (see also **Cahirciveen** page 79).
Signposted off the N70, 1.5km north of Caherdaniel. Tel: 066–75113. Open: April and October, Tuesday to Sunday 1–5pm; May to September, Monday to Saturday 9am–6pm, Sunday 11am–7pm. Last admission 45 minutes before closing. Admission charge to house; grounds freely accessible.

DUNBEG FORT

Perched on a promontory high above Dingle Bay, this Iron Age fort is protected on its landward side by trenches and a 7m-thick wall. The circular fort itself, now ruined, also has thick walls.
On the R559 near Fahan, about 6km west of Ventry. Freely accessible.

GALLARUS ORATORY

Amazingly pristine, the oratory is a perfect example of early Irish building, dating from the 8th or possibly the 7th century. Completely unmortared, it has remained watertight for 1,200 years.
Off the R559, between Ballyferriter and Ballynana. Freely accessible.

KERRY THE KINGDOM

A 'time car' trip back to medieval Tralee, along a reconstructed street and into houses peopled with life-like models in authentic dress, this attraction

BEEHIVE HUTS

More than 400 *clochans* – beehive-shaped stone cells – are to be found on the southern slopes of Mount Eagle. Although unmortared, the prehistoric structures are quite watertight, and in early Christian times were used by hermit monks. The greatest concentration of huts is on the R559 between Slea Head and Dunquin, many in fields and farmyards.

Shaped like an upturned boat, Gallarus Oratory has stood the test of time

incorporates Kerry County Museum, which outlines 7,000 years of the area's history.

Ashe Memorial Hall, Denny Street, Tralee. Tel: 066–27777. Open: Monday to Saturday 10am–8pm, Sunday 2–6pm. Admission charge.

KILMALKEDAR CHURCH

This ruined 12th-century church is a fine example of Romanesque architecture. The narrow east window is known locally as 'the eye of the needle' through which those seeking salvation must pass. The Alphabet Stone, a pillar standing inside the church, is inscribed with both Roman and ancient Irish characters.

Off the R559, near the Gallarus Oratory. Freely accessible.

MUCKROSS ABBEY AND HOUSE

Despite vandalism by Cromwell's troops in 1652, which left it roofless, the 15th-century Franciscan abbey remains in a surprisingly good state of preservation. Visitors can climb ancient stone stairs to examine the monks' living quarters, kitchen and refectory.

Not far from the abbey is Muckross

House. Surrounded by landscaped gardens noted for rhododendrons and azaleas, it was built in the 19th century in Elizabethan style. Its upper floors house a collection of maps, prints and other documents and there is a small wildlife and bird exhibition. The house also incorporates the Kerry Folklife Centre with a country pub, print shop, dairy and carpenter's shop. Craftspeople demonstrate weaving, basket-making, pottery and smithying. There is an exhibition of old agricultural implements and machinery, and another display illustrates Kerry's musical and poetic heritage.

On the N71 Kenmare road, 4km outside Killarney. Abbey open: daily during daylight hours. Free. House – tel: 064–31440. Open: 17 March to end June and September to October, daily 9am–6pm; July and August, daily 9am–7pm; rest of year, daily 11am–5pm. Admission charge, gardens free.

SKELLIG EXPERIENCE

This interpretative centre explores the history and archaeology of Skellig Michael's Early Christian monastery, its lighthouse service, and local wildlife.
Valentina Island, by road bridge from Portmagee. Tel: 066–76306. Open: mid-April to end September, daily 10am–7pm. Admission charge.

CO LIMERICK
FOYNES FLYING BOAT MUSEUM

The focal point for aircraft crossing the north Atlantic in the 1930s and 1940s, the old terminus building, radio and weather rooms are on show, with original equipment. An audio-visual presentation is given in a 1940s-style cinema and there is a tea room of the same era.
On the N69, about 24km west of Limerick. Tel: 069–65416. Open: April to October, daily 10am–6pm. Admission charge.

KING JOHN'S CASTLE

Imaginative models and displays interpret Limerick's 800-year history in the city's restored 13th-century castle. Battlement walkways along the castle walls and towers provide wonderful views of the city, the River Shannon and surrounding countryside.
Castle Street, Limerick. Tel: 061–411201/2. Open: daily 9.30am–5.30pm. Admission charge.

LOUGH GUR STONE AGE CENTRE

The area around Lough Gur is one of Ireland's most important archaeological sites, with numerous megalithic remains – stone circles, dolmens, wedge-shaped gallery graves and the sites of neolithic dwellings. A wealth of artefacts has been discovered in and around the lake. An audio-visual presentation of the Lough Gur story is given in the 'neolithic-style' Stone Age Interpretative Centre.
Signposted 17km south of Limerick off the R512 to Kilmallock. Tel: 061–85186. Open: May to September, daily 10am–1pm, 2–6pm. Admission charge.

Charming 15th-century carved choir stalls, St Mary's Cathedral

ST MARY'S CATHEDRAL

Built as a palace in the 12th century, the cathedral (Protestant) still shows original architectural features. Misericords in the choir stalls, dating from the 15th century, bear grotesque carvings. During summer months St Mary's is the setting for a colourful *son et lumière* show highlighting dramatic moments in the city's history.
Bridge Street, Limerick. Tel: 061–461238. Freely accessible. Son et lumière: mid-June to mid-September, nightly 7pm and 9.15pm. Admission charge.

CO CLARE

AILLWEE CAVE

Hollows scraped out on the floor of the huge cave provide evidence of early occupation by the brown bear, which once prowled in the area surrounding The Burren. The cave, one of the oldest in Ireland estimated at two million years old, has a river, a waterfall and 1km of well-lit passages. Entry is through an award-winning visitor centre built into the hillside.

3km south of Ballyvaughan (signposted). Tel: 065–77036. Open: mid-March to early November, daily 10am–dusk. Last tour: July and August, 6.30pm; rest of year, 5.30pm. Admission charge.

BUNRATTY CASTLE AND FOLK PARK

A restored Norman-Irish keep built in 1277, the castle houses a fine collection of furniture and furnishings from the 14th to the 17th centuries. Medieval banquets are a twice-nightly feature throughout the year. The Folk Park, in the castle grounds, is a reconstructed 19th-century street, with craft shops, general stores and post office. Traditional crafts are seen in action, and country meals are served in a barn restaurant.

On the N18, 12km northwest of Limerick. Tel: 061–361511. Open: daily 9.30am–5pm (until 7pm June to August). Last admission to castle, 4.30pm. Admission charge.

CRAGGAUNOWEN HISTORICAL PROJECT

Many skills of the distant past have been revived in this progressive project in the grounds of a restored 16th-century castle. The most dramatic reconstruction is that of a *crannog*, a Bronze Age lake dwelling. The replica of St Brendan's 6th-century leather boat, in which Tim Severin crossed the Atlantic, is also on show.

Off the R469, 10km south of Quin. Tel: 061–367178. Open: May to September, daily 10am–6pm. Admission charge.

Bunratty Folk Park – a living museum of traditional village life

Cork City

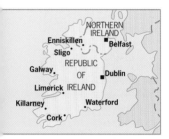

Cork is built on an island embraced by two channels of the River Lee. The city's twisting, hilly streets and narrow lanes create traffic delays at times, so walking is the best way to get around. There is much to enjoy in a city which has retained some of the old ambience of a tall ships port. *Allow 1½ hours.*

Begin at St Patrick's Bridge. Proceed right along Lavitt's Quay. Opposite Opera House Bridge turn left into Emmet Place.

1 EMMET PLACE

The concrete drabness of Cork's Opera House may come as a disappointment, but the theatre offers a full programme of classical and popular opera, ballet and drama. The adjacent Crawford Municipal Art Gallery has an extensive collection of local landscapes from the 18th and 19th centuries. Exhibitions by contemporary Irish and international artists are also staged.
At the bottom of Emmet Place continue west along Paul Street.

2 PAUL STREET

Pedestrianised Paul Street has brought new life to the city centre, with restaurants, boutiques, art and craft studios, and street entertainment in an attractive piazza. Traditional

Nearby

7 City Hall

Cork – a delightful waterside city connected by bridges across the River Lee

Irish goods are available in the shops.
Continue west to the junction of Cornmarket Street and Castle Street.

3 CORNMARKET STREET
Coal Quay market stands at the junction and is the survivor of an open-air market that once continued along the length of Cornmarket Street. Today, the bulk of the area's trade is in second-hand clothing and antiques.
Follow Castle Street, turning left at North Main Street and right into Washington Street. At Grattan Street turn left, cross Clarke's Bridge and turn right on to Wandesford Quay, following Sharman Crawford Street to Bishop Street.

4 ST FINN BARRE'S CATHEDRAL
The cathedral's three spires give it a medieval look, but the building dates from the 19th century. Belonging to the Church of Ireland, it stands on the site of a monastery founded by St Finbarr in 650 (see page 71).
Follow Bishop Street to Proby's Quay, re-crossing the river at South Gate Bridge.

5 SOUTH MAIN STREET
South Main Street leads to two further centres of art and culture. Bishop Lucey Park, on the right, has a permanent exhibition of modern Cork sculpture. Also on the right, narrow Tobin Street leads to the Triskel Arts Centre, with exhibitions of contemporary arts and crafts, as well as film shows and stage productions.
Follow Tobin Street to Grand Parade.

6 GRAND PARADE
Spacious Grand Parade runs from crescent-shaped St Patrick's Street, Cork's main thoroughfare, to the south channel of the River Lee. About halfway along – close to where Tobin Street emerges – is the entrance to the English Market, a covered area of traditional stalls selling fish, meat, fruit and vegetables. At its southern end, the Parade has a monument to Irish patriots of the 18th and 19th centuries.
Turn left into South Mall.

7 SOUTH MALL
The start of South Mall is marked by a memorial to the Royal Munster Fusiliers who fell in World War I. Across the road, the roof of the Allied Irish Bank is supported by six marble pillars from Old St Paul's, London.
Turn left into Princes Street and right into St Patrick's Street, completing the walk at St Patrick's Bridge.

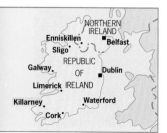

The Ring of Kerry

Justifiably the most popular excursion in Ireland, the 170km Ring of Kerry is a dramatic experience: a mix of rugged moorland and mountains, lakes, rivers and streams, cliffs, beaches and weatherbeaten islands. *Allow 1 day.*

Begin at the town of Killarney.

1 KILLARNEY

A comparatively modern resort – it sprang into prominence when 18th-century tourists were drawn to its wonderful setting – Killarney is a lively place where jaunting cars and coaches compete in busy streets. St Mary's Cathedral, completed in 1885, is the work of flamboyant architect Augustus Pugin.
Follow the N71 southwest for 18km to Ladies' View.

Nearby

1 Muckross Abbey and House (see page 73)
6 Derrynane House (see page 72)

2 LADIES' VIEW

The road soon weaves and climbs above the waters of Muckross Lake, and it is not difficult to understand the delight of Queen Victoria and her ladies-in-waiting, after whom the view is named. It is best seen from the second car park – a great panorama of the Killarney Valley.

Continue along the N71 for 5km.

3 MOLL'S GAP
Another stunning viewpoint overlooks
Macgillycuddy's Reeks and 1,041m-high
Carrauntoohill, Ireland's highest
mountain. The rounded rocks were
formed by glacial action. Moll's Gap has
a restaurant and craft shop.
Continue south for 10km to Kenmare.

4 KENMARE
The streets of Kenmare, reached after a
drive across rugged mountain terrain,
were laid out in an X-formation in 1775
by the first Marquess of Lansdowne. The
town has an ancient stone circle, known
locally as the Druid's Circle, on the
banks of the River Finnihy.
Take the N70 west for 27km to Sneem.

5 SNEEM
The road follows the Kenmare River,
and there are splendid views of the Caha
and Slieve Miskish Mountains. Sneem,
a pretty village with colourful houses
surrounding a green, has good safe
beaches. Fishing for salmon and brown
trout is popular.

Four kilometres inland from
Castlecove, on the N70, is Staigue
Fort, about 2,500 years old and one
of Ireland's best-preserved ancient
structures.
Continue on the N70 for 35km to
Waterville.

6 WATERVILLE
Waterville, best known today for its
championship golf course and salmon
fishing, is said to be the landing place
of Noah's grandson Beith and
granddaughter Cessair, who had failed
to gain places on the Ark and had to
build their own.

Jaunting car rides are a popular way to enjoy
the delights of Killarney town

Drive north for 16km to Cahirciveen.

7 CAHIRCIVEEN
South Kerry's major shopping town,
Cahirciveen is a place with strong
associations with the patriot Daniel
O'Connell. The Liberator's birthplace,
ruined Carhan House, is 1.5km north of
the town. The town is also the terminus
for a ferry service to Valentia Island,
which has nothing but 3,000km of ocean
between it and Newfoundland (see also
Skellig Experience page 74).
Follow the N70 for another 40km to
Killorglin.

8 KILLORGLIN
The road skirts Dingle Bay, with views
to the north of the Dingle Peninsula's
peaks, and passes through the resort of
Glenbeigh. Killorglin, a hillside town, is
best known for its mid-August Puck Fair,
a three-day festival based on the pagan
custom of crowning a billy goat as King.
Take the R562 southeast for 21km to
complete the drive at Killarney.

Connacht

*C*onnacht, where Irish is a living language and University College Galway is a centre of Gaelic culture, has a range of beautiful scenery – from tranquil to wild and craggy. Its lakes and the shore of the River Shannon attract thousands of fishermen every year, and its extensive coastline caters for the sea angler, the yachtsman and the beach addict.

Lively Galway City combines a medieval atmosphere with a musical and cultural tradition which draws in young people from Europe and beyond each summer. Thousands more pour into Knock as pilgrims, worshipping in a church built in the 1970s to accommodate 20,000.

CO GALWAY
ALCOCK AND BROWN MEMORIAL

A cairn near the Marconi station ruins (see page 82) marks the place where intrepid aviators Alcock and Brown landed after the first non-stop transatlantic flight from St John's, Newfoundland, in 1919. On higher ground an aircraft monument marks the achievement.

Derrygimlagh Bog, 6km south of Clifden. Freely accessible.

ARAN ISLANDS

See pages 126–7.

AUGHNANURE CASTLE

Close to the shores of Lough Corrib, on rocky ground, this well-preserved 16th-century Irish tower house, built by the O'Flahertys, stands six storeys high. The remains of a banqueting hall, a circular watch-tower and a dry harbour can be seen.

Oughterard. Tel: 091–82214. Open: mid-June to mid-September, daily 10am–6pm. Admission charge.

CONNEMARA NATIONAL PARK

This 2,000-hectare area encompasses a range of habitats – heath, bogland, woodland and grassland – including four peaks of the Twelve Bens (Pins) mountain range. There are stunning views and a well-established herd of Connemara ponies roams the park. The visitor centre provides detailed information on a variety of walks and nature trails.

Letterfrack, western Co Galway. Visitor Centre – tel: 095–41054. Open: May to September, daily 10am–6.30pm. Admission charge.

Ashleagh waterfall, near Lean, in Connemara

COOLE NATURE RESERVE

The grounds of Lady Augusta Gregory's former estate, Coole Park, have now become a nature reserve. This unique matrix of habitats, which incorporates a nature trail, a forest walk and a lake, is home to a fine herd of red deer and a wide variety of other animal and bird species. There is an interpretative centre which explains the role of the reserve, as well as picnic sites and tea rooms.
Gort. Tel: 091–31804. Open: daily until dusk. Admission charge.

KYLEMORE ABBEY

This attractive lakeside abbey, originally built as a public residence, is now a convent for Benedictine nuns. Its Gothic chapel is a small-scale version of England's Norwich Cathedral. The well-stocked craft shop sells hand-crafted pottery and there is a restaurant run by the nuns.
Connemara. Tel: 095–41146. Abbey open: mid-March to October, 10am–6pm. Grounds open: February to Christmas Eve, 10am–6pm. Free.

CONNACHT

MARCONI WIRELESS STATION

Only the foundations and some of the masts remain of the first transatlantic wireless station, established by the Marconi company. The station was destroyed during fighting in the Irish Civil War (1922–3).
Derrygimlagh Bog, 6km south of Clifden. Freely accessible.

PORTUMNA WILDLIFE SANCTUARY

Portumna Forest Park, run by the Forest and Wildlife Service, has 400 hectares of walks in what was formerly the Harewood Estate. Bordered along its southern edges by Lough Derg, the sanctuary is home to a variety of animals, including red and fallow deer. A nature trail leaflet is available.
Near Portumna town, approaching from Woodford. Freely accessible.

SKY DRIVE

The Sky Drive, 14km of narrow road high over Clifden Bay, is one of the most scenic stretches of Co Galway, circling the peninsula west of the town and opening up vast seacapes. This road is very popular with landscape painters.

THOOR BALLYLEE

This former summer house of W B Yeats, where he wrote most of his works, has been restored to look as it did in his time. The 16th-century tower house contains a display of first editions of his work and visitors can 'climb the narrow, winding stair'. There is an audio-visual presentation of the poet's life, as well as a bookshop, craft shop, tea room, gardens and picnic area.
Gort. Tel: 091–31436. Open: Easter to September, daily 10am–6pm. Admission charge.

The Turoe Stone, enigmatic, but possibly a component in ancient fertility rites

TUROE STONE

Believed to date from the first century, this large granite boulder, standing in a field, is a rare example of a decorated Celtic pillar stone, with fine La Tène sculpting.
5km north of Loughrea, near Bullaun. Freely accessible.

CO MAYO
ACHILL ISLAND

Reached by a short causeway, Achill Island is the largest of Ireland's islands. Its economy depends largely on tourism as little of the island's 15,000 hectares can be cultivated – it is mostly mountain or bogland covered in heather. There are weird rock formations in the cliffs flanking the 3km beach at Keel, and the Atlantic Drive provides excellent views of the foothills and sandy beaches.

Boats can be hired at Keel Harbour for shark and other big-game fishing or to enjoy the dramatic cliff scenery. Stone circles and dolmens are dotted about inland.
Reached from Mulrany on the mainland.

ASHFORD CASTLE

Formerly a home of the Guinness family, this turreted castle, set on the shores of Lough Corrib, is now one of Ireland's most luxurious hotels. Its prestigious guest-list includes former US President, Ronald Reagan. The village of Cong was used as the location for the 1951 John Wayne film, *The Quiet Man*. *Cong. Tel: 092–46003. Free.*

CÉIDE FIELDS

An environmental interpretive centre, with audio-visual presentations, opened in 1992 at this extensive Stone Age settlement, where tombs, 5000-year-old dwellings, rare plants and rock formations can be seen.
8km west of Ballycastle. Tel: 096–43325. Open: mid-March to early May, daily 10am–5pm; June to September, daily 9.30am– 6.30pm; October and November, daily 10am–5pm. Guided tours of site. Admission charge.

CLARE ISLAND

See page 127.

CONG ABBEY

Completed in 1120 for the Augustinians, Cong Abbey replaced a former church built in 623 and destroyed by the Norsemen. It was founded by Turlough Mor O'Conor, High King of Ireland, whose son, Rory, destined to be the last High King, died in the abbey in 1198. The restored cloister and the monks' fishing house, built on a river platform, can still be seen. The abbey was an important ecclesiastical centre for more than 700 years, and some 3,000 people once lived there. The last Abbot of Cong died in 1829.
Cong, between Lough Mask and Lough Corrib. Freely accessible.

The excellent sandy beach on Achill, Ireland's largest island

FOXFORD WOOLLEN MILLS VISITOR CENTRE

The story of this 19th-century working mill, from the famine years to the present day, is told in an animated presentation. *Foxford. Tel: 094–56756. Open: May to October, Monday to Saturday 10am–6pm, Sunday noon–6pm; November to April, Monday to Saturday 10am–6pm, Sunday 2–6pm. Admission charge.*

INISHKEA ISLANDS

These two low-lying, exposed islands form a sanctuary for up to 60 per cent of the Irish winter population of barnacle geese – some 2,900 birds. There are also early Christian remains connected with St Columba here.
4km west of Mullet Peninsula.

Thousands visit Knock's shrine every year

KNOCK SHRINE

Pilgrims from around the world flock to Knock, where apparitions of the Virgin Mary were reported in 1879. Since then it has been regarded as the Lourdes of Ireland. A 20,000-seat circular church was built at the site in 1976 to accommodate the huge pilgrimages. Its finest hour came when Pope John Paul II visited the site in 1979.
On the N17, 15km south of Horan (Knock) International Airport. Freely accessible.

WESTPORT HOUSE

One of the most stately homes of Ireland, this handsome Georgian mansion, begun in 1730, was completed in 1788 for the Marquess of Sligo on the site of an earlier castle whose dungeons still exist. The architect was Richard Cassels, whose work was re-modelled by James Wyatt. It is a place of contrasts – antique silver, Waterford glass, Georgian and Victorian furniture, and family portraits by Reynolds are on display, while video games flash in the dungeons. A children's amusement park is set up in the small lakeside grounds.
The Quay, Westport. Tel: 098–25141. Open: late May and late August to mid-September, Monday to Saturday 2–5pm; June, Monday to Saturday 2–6pm; July to late August, Monday to Saturday 10.30am–6pm, Sunday 2–6pm. Admission charge.

WESTPORT TOWN

With an octagonal centre, lime trees lining either side of a canalised river, Clew Bay at its feet and a wealth of grand Georgian buildings, the planned town of Westport attracts many visitors. The Thursday morning market at the Octagon brings the farmers into town, and there is a frenzy of buying and selling at the clothes, produce and novelty stalls. It is even more lively when the annual Street Festival takes place in the second week of July, with free music concerts and street entertainment. At the end of September there is an arts festival.

CO SLIGO
CARROWMORE
The largest cemetery of megalithic tombs in Ireland can be seen at the top of a mountain at Carrowmore. More than 60 tombs, a variety of dolmens, passage graves and stone circles extend for 3km. One of the dolmens dates back to 4000BC, while the Bronze Age standing stones are thought to be from 1750BC. The fact that all the tombs are built to the same pattern suggests Carrowmore may have been a battle site.
Southeast of Knocknarea Hill, on the R292. Freely accessible.

CAVES OF KEAGH
Seventeen small caves on the western side of a mountain show traces of human occupation, and the remains of cave bears, Arctic lemmings, Irish elk and reindeer were also discovered. According to legend, it was in one of these caves that Cormac Mac Airt, King of Cashel, was reared by a she-wolf.
On the R295, 10km south of Ballymote. Freely accessible.

DRUMCLIFF MONASTIC SITE
Little is left of this 6th-century settlement except the stump of a round tower on one side of the N15 road and an elaborately carved 1,000-year-old high cross on the other. The carvings on either side of the cross depict a selection of biblical scenes from Adam and Eve to the Crucifixion (see page 95).
Drumcliff, 8km north of Sligo. Freely accessible.

Westport has a rich legacy of fine town houses and spacious streets

COUNTRY LIFE

Rural life is *the* way of life to a large proportion of Irish people. Apart from the conurbations with six-figure populations – Dublin, Cork, Limerick and Belfast – towns are small islands of activity in a brilliant green landscape, where agriculture makes a vital contribution to the economy.

In the Republic some 5¹/₂ million of the country's 7 million hectares are devoted to agriculture, and about 14 per cent of the workforce is directly involved in it.

Farming, forestry and fishing are important industries in Northern Ireland. So it is no surprise that such events as show jumping, horse-racing, agricultural shows and ploughing matches attract huge numbers of spectators or that hunting, shooting and fishing are pursuits enjoyed by many thousands.

Small fields enclosed by low stone walls give way to open bogland, rich reddish-brown, or tiny rural main road villages. Barley, wheat, sugar beet and potatoes grow well in the rich, moist soil, but it is sheep and cattle rearing and dairy products that represent most of the agricultural output. Even on busy main roads motorists must be prepared to encounter a herd of cows or flock of sheep.

Living in isolated farms and cottages, the people are nevertheless gregarious, enjoying the social, sporting and cultural life to be found in bars and church halls, dance halls and playing fields.

On market days the country goes to town. Jam-packed at the bar after

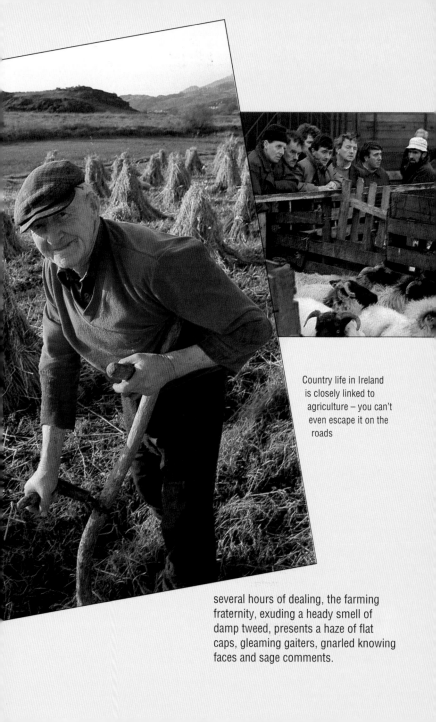

Country life in Ireland is closely linked to agriculture – you can't even escape it on the roads

several hours of dealing, the farming fraternity, exuding a heady smell of damp tweed, presents a haze of flat caps, gleaming gaiters, gnarled knowing faces and sage comments.

HAZELWOOD SCULPTURE TRAIL

A unique collection of wooden sculptures are dispersed throughout Hazelwood Forest, on the northern shore of Lough Gill. The sculptures range from figures from Irish legend to art nouveau forms by Irish and foreign sculptors, and can be seen by following forest trails starting at the car park.
3km from Sligo, off the Dromahair road. Freely accessible.

INNISCRONE (ENNISCRONE)

Seaweed found at this seaside resort, 53km west of Sligo, by Killala Bay, is renowned for its curative properties. People travel from far and wide to submerge themselves in the hot, seaweed-enriched salt water at the town's bath houses. Just north of the town is the Valley of Diamonds – a shell collector's paradise.

Kilkullen, Inniscrone. Opening times vary: check tourist office for details (tel: 096–36202). Admission charge.

INNISFREE

There are boat trips from Sligo Town to the Lough Gill island immortalised by the poet Yeats. But those content to look from further afield can see it from the shore.
Lough Gill, east of Sligo. Freely accessible.

LISSADELL HOUSE

Lissadell House is the home of the distinguished Gore-Booth family, two of whom – Eva and Constance – were friends of W B Yeats. He wrote a poem to them, *In Memory of Eva Gore-Booth and Con Markievicz* which is on display by the main gate. The contents of the house reflect the colourful lives led by the family.

Part of the estate is a forestry, wildlife

Left: Lissadell – home of the Gore-Booths

and bird reserve, known locally as the 'Goose Field' because it has Ireland's largest colony of barnacle geese – immigrants from Greenland. The key to a hide, from which a variety of birds may be observed, is available from the reserve warden. Large numbers of seals can sometimes be seen basking on a sand-bank in the nearby bay.
Signposted from the N51 at Carney. Tel: 071–63150. Open: June to September, Monday to Saturday 10.30am–noon, 2–4.30pm. Admission charge.

STRANDHILL

Strandhill is a quiet seaside village with a good beach, sand dunes and excellent facilities for surfing, but swimming is not always safe. A flag system indicates danger and a beach guard is on duty in summer.

Dolly's Cottage, a small folk museum housed in a 19th-century dwelling, sells home-made produce and occasionally holds evening folk music sessions.
Strandhill, near Sligo Airport. Dolly's Cottage open: July and August, daily 3–5pm.

YEATS' GRAVE

Though he died in Roquebrune, France, W B Yeats was eventually buried at Drumcliff. Tidily maintained, the plain grave of the poet lies within the shadow of the flat-topped Benbulben Mountain. The headstone bears an inscription from his final poem:
Cast a cold eye
On life, on death.
Horseman, pass by!
Drumcliff Churchyard, on the N15 north of Sligo. Freely accessible.

CO ROSCOMMON
BOYLE ABBEY

The impressive ruins of this Cistercian abbey show traces of their original splendour. The nave, with both Romanesque and Gothic arches, and the choir and transepts of the 12th-century church are still in good condition.
Boyle. Tel: 079–62604. Open: mid-June to mid-September, daily 9.30am–1.30pm, 2.30–6.30pm. Admission charge.

CLONALIS HOUSE

Clonalis is the ancestral home of the clan O'Conor, who claim to be Europe's oldest family, tracing their ancestry to AD75. The 19th-century mansion contains many items associated with the family, including the harp of Ireland's last great bard, Turlough O'Carolan (1630–1738).
Castlerea. Tel: 0907–20014. Open: June to mid-September, Tuesday to Sunday noon–5pm. Admission charge.

> Castlerea is Co Roscommon's third largest town, and is known mainly as the birthplace, in 1815, of Sir William Wilde, the father of Oscar.

FUERTY

In the graveyard are the ruins of a Franciscan church in which 100 priests were killed by a local tyrant, Robert Ormsby, at the time of Cromwell's plundering. Carvings on the headstone of a blacksmith's grave show the tools of his trade – anvil, bellows and tongs, while a shepherd's headstone depicts sheep and a crook. The county's economy is still based on sheep and cattle, and Roscommon has one of Ireland's leading weekly livestock markets.
5km southwest of Roscommon.

ROSCOMMON

All the public hangings in Co Roscommon took place at Roscommon Gaol. One of the inmates long ago, the notorious 'Lady Betty' was found guilty of the murder of her son, but had her death sentence commuted on condition that she carried out all further hangings without fee or reward. She accepted the deal, which is commemorated with a plaque. The 18th-century gaol fell into disuse in 1822. Part of the solid stone wall of the gaol has been incorporated into a development of shops.

Roscommon's Norman castle was built, captured by the Irish who razed it to the ground, and re-built all in the space of 11 years, from 1269 to 1280. Massive and roofless, though otherwise reasonably well preserved, it stands sombrely north of town.

Just out of town, on the road to Boyle, is the impressive ruin of Roscommon Abbey. This Dominican priory was founded in 1253 and somehow survived the religious persecution following the Reformation. Eight sculpted figures can be seen at the base of the tomb of Felim O'Conor, King of Connacht, in the remains of a substantial church. They depict gallowglasses – medieval Irish professional soldiers.
Roscommon.

CO LEITRIM

Leitrim is Ireland's least populated county. Its largest town, Carrick-on-Shannon, has a population of fewer than 2,000. Anglers appreciate its many lakes and rivers, including a large section of the Shannon.

CO LEITRIM
FENAGH

It is believed that the small village of Fenagh was thickly populated in pre-Christian times because of the number of megalithic burial chambers.
Near Ballinamore.

GLENCAR WATERFALL

From the N16 Manorhamilton to Sligo road you will see the 17m-high waterfall tumbling in an unbroken leap into Glencar Lough long before the right turn that leads you to it. There are several waterfalls near by, but this is the highest. Yeats immortalised it in his poem *The Stolen Child*.
East of Drumcliff. Freely accessible.

Lough Key is the star attraction in the picturesque forest park

Sturdy Parke's Castle offers a superb view over the lovely Lough Gill

KILTYCLOGHER

Sean MacDiarmada, who was executed in Dublin for his part in the 1916 Easter Rising, was born here. His statue stands in the village.
Northeast of Manorhamilton.

KINLOUGH FOLK MUSEUM

Kinlough's folk museum may be small, but it is crammed with fascinating items – documents, household and agricultural artefacts and a whiskey still.
Barrack Street, Kinlough. No telephone. Key from the grocer's shop opposite. Free.

LOUGH KEY FOREST PARK

A few kilometres from the county capital, Carrick-on-Shannon, this forest park lies along the banks of Lough Key. It has nature trails, bog gardens, a deer enclosure and boating facilities.
Freely accessible. Charge for car park.

LOUGH RINN HOUSE AND GARDENS

This estate was the ancestral home of the Earls of Leitrim. The 1.5-hectare walled garden, designed in 1859, was originally laid out to supply the house with fruit and vegetables and has been extensively replanted in the manner of a Victorian pleasure garden. It is divided into three distinct sections: formal bedding in the top garden; herbaceous borders with an orange, yellow, silver and white theme in the middle; and a mixed perennial and shrub border.
Mohill. Tel: 078–31427. Open: April to September, daily 10am–7pm. Last tour 5.30pm. Admission charge.

PARKE'S CASTLE

This strongly fortified 17th-century house was the home of an Englishman named Parke, who undiplomatically dismantled a neighbouring castle to provide the material to build his own. The castle had been owned by the powerful O'Rourke clan, and as a result Parke's home needed to be impregnable as a defence against the outraged Irish. A video presentation relates the story, and there is a guided tour (see page 95).
Near Sligo, on the north shore of Lough Gill. Tel: 071–64149. Open: June to September, daily 9.30am–6pm; mid-April to May and October, Tuesday to Sunday 10am–5pm. Admission charge.

Galway City

Prosperous, vibrant and compact, historic Galway is ideal for touring on foot. *Allow 1½ hours.*

Begin on the southeast side of Eyre Square, in front of the Great Southern Hotel (the rail and bus stations are behind the hotel, on Station Road).

1 EYRE SQUARE

The square is surrounded by Galway's liveliest pubs and eating places. Its central area – Kennedy Park – is the setting for outdoor performances during the city's many festivals. The 6m steel sculpture, the work of Eamonn O'Donnel, symbolises the Galway 'hookers', traditional ships that once plied Galway Bay.

Nearby

6 St Nicholas' Cathedral

From the square's northwest corner follow Williamsgate Street to William Street and continue to Abbeygate Street.

2 LYNCH'S CASTLE

The Allied Irish Bank on the corner of Shop Street and Abbeygate Street is the best-preserved example of a merchant's town castle. Believed to have been built in the reign of Henry VIII, it features impressive coats-of-arms and fine fireplaces.

Turn right into Abbeygate Street and left into Market Street.

3 LYNCH MEMORIAL

An inscription on black marble set above a Gothic doorway marks the spot where, so local legend says, a 16th-century mayor of Galway found his own son guilty of murder, then hanged the boy himself when the executioner refused to carry out the sentence.

Continue to Lombard Street.

4 COLLEGIATE CHURCH OF ST NICHOLAS

Built by the Anglo-Normans in 1320 and enlarged in the 15th and 16th centuries, the church has many fine medieval carvings and relics and a peal of eight bells. A colourful street market spills around the church on Saturdays.

Take Bowling Green.

5 NORA BARNACLE'S HOME

A memorial plaque marks the former home of Nora Barnacle, James Joyce's wife. It was unveiled in 1982 to mark the centenary of his birth. The house is open to the public (Monday to Saturday, admission charge).

At the end of Bowling Green turn left into Newton Smith and continue to where Salmon Weir Bridge crosses the River Corrib.

Memorial to the plucky salmon

6 SALMON WEIR BRIDGE

Galway's best-known attraction, the bridge is the place from which shoals of salmon can be seen as they make their way upstream to spawn from mid-April to early July.

Follow the signed riverside walk to William O'Brien's Bridge, bear left along Bridge Street, right into Cross Street, and right into Quay Street to the Spanish Arch.

7 SPANISH ARCH

Built in 1594, the arch once protected the quays on which Spanish galleons unloaded. Today, it adjoins the Galway City Museum. Claddagh, viewed across the River Corrib, is the former fishing village where the traditional Irish wedding ring is said to have originated.

Return along Quay Street through the shopping area of High Street and Shop Street to complete the walk at Eyre Square.

Yeats Country

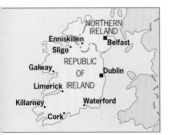

The distinctive profile of Benbulben broods over Sligo Bay and appears unexpectedly, ever changing in the area's capricious climate. The drive embraces some of the places where the poet W B Yeats found inspiration. *Allow 1 day.*

Begin at Sligo Town.

1 SLIGO, CO SLIGO

Sligo has a long and often violent history. In the 9th century it was attacked by the Vikings, followed by Irish and Anglo-Norman raiders. Its population was reduced by a third during Ireland's great famine. The only remains of its early days are the ruins of the 13th-century Dominican abbey in Abbey Street. Sligo County Library and Museum has many paintings by W B Yeats' father, John, and his brother, Jack. W B himself (1865–1939) is commemorated in the Yeats Building where an

Nearby

2 Lissadell House
  (see pages 88–9)

annual Yeats Summer School is held each August. The Fiddler of Dooney competition, inspired by his poem, takes place at Sligo every July to choose Ireland's champion fiddler.
Take the N15 for 8km to Drumcliff.

2 DRUMCLIFF, CO SLIGO

The stump of a round tower and a thousand-year-old high cross are all that remain of a monastery thought to have been founded by St Columba in the 6th century (see page 85). Yeats's simple grave is to the left of the entrance to the rather grim Protestant church.
Continue on the N15 for 37km to Bundoran, then take the R280 for 5km to Kinlough.

3 KINLOUGH, CO LEITRIM

An attractive village with excellent coarse and salmon fishing facilities, Kinlough overlooks Lough Melvin and the ruins of Rossclogher Abbey.
Follow the R281 along the south shore of Lough Melvin for 13km, then turn right on to the R282 and continue for the same distance to Manorhamilton.

4 MANORHAMILTON, CO LEITRIM

This workaday community was named after a 17th-century Scottish 'planter', Sir Frederick Hamilton, who built the now ruined castle overlooking the town.
Follow the N16 west for about 13km to Glencar Lake.

5 GLENCAR, CO LEITRIM

The N16 skirts the lake, presenting superb alpine views of the Glencar Waterfall immortalised in Yeats' poem, *The Stolen Child* (see page 90). The Glencar Valley is an ecological pot-pourri, with mixed woodland and

rare species of plant life.
Continue along the N16 for about 16km, then turn left to Parke's Castle Visitor Centre on the R286.

Yeats, leader of the Irish literary revival and co-founder of Dublin's Abbey Theatre

6 PARKE'S CASTLE, CO LEITRIM

An impressively reconstructed manor house, Parke's Castle offers a superb view of Lough Gill, strewn with islands and surrounded by ancient woodland (see page 91).
Continue on the R286, then turn right on the R288 for Dromahair.

7 DROMAHAIR, CO LEITRIM

Dromahair hosts gatherings of the O'Rourke family. The village was laid out along the lines of a Somerset settlement by an English family, the Lane-Foxes. From here, you can take a boat to Yeats' Lake Isle of Innisfree.
Take the R287 west for 16km to Dooney.

8 DOONEY, CO SLIGO

Dooney Rock Forest is in a beautiful corner of Lough Gill. Here are the 'twining branches' mentioned in Yeats' poem *The Fiddler of Dooney*.
From Dooney take the N4 north to complete the drive at Sligo.

Ulster

*T*he ancient province of Ulster encompasses not only the six counties of Northern Ireland, but also Donegal, Cavan and Monaghan in the Republic. There is much to see – the incredibly beautiful Sperrin Mountains, the Antrim Coast Road and the glorious lakeland of Fermanagh, or travel across country to Londonderry and Donegal where beauty is revealed round every corner.

BELFAST
BELFAST ZOO
On the lower slopes of Cave Hill, overlooking the city, the zoo has a lake with flamingos, and a *crannog*, or fortified lake dwelling. There are red pandas, spectacular bears, rare tamarins and marmosets, sea lions and penguins.
Antrim Road, 6.5km north of Belfast. Tel: 01232–776277. Open: daily 10am– 5pm (to 3.30pm, except Friday to 2.30pm, October to March). Admission charge.

BOTANIC GARDENS
Dominated by the elegant covered-glass and cast-iron Victorian Palm House, these pleasant gardens include a Tropical Ravine where many of the plants enclosed are a century old.
Stranmillis Road, Belfast 7. Tel: 01232– 324902. Open: daily dawn–dusk. Palm House and Tropical Ravine: Monday to Friday 10am–5pm, weekends and public holidays 2–5pm (to 4pm daily October to March); closed daily for lunch. Free.

CAVE HILL COUNTRY PARK
At the top of Cave Hill is MacArt's Fort, ancient earthworks where, in 1798, Wolfe Tone and United Irishmen colleagues asserted their independence from England. On the lower slopes, the impressive 19th-century Belfast Castle, contains a heritage centre.
6.5km north of Belfast. Freely accessible. Heritage Centre open: daily 9am–6pm. Free.

CITY HALL

Just a village in the 17th century, by 1888 Belfast had nearly 300,000 people, and Queen Victoria gave it city status. Work began on the ornate City Hall, built in classical style with a high dome based on St Paul's Cathedral in London. It opened in 1906 (see page 116). *Donegall Square, Belfast 1. Tel: 01232–320202, ext 2618. Tours: July to September, Monday to Friday 10am and 2.30pm; October to June, Wednesday 10am. Free.*

ULSTER

The unusual Sinclair Seamen's Church, with its unmistakable maritime atmosphere

CROWN LIQUOR SALOON

This ornately decorated, former railway hotel, with its gas lighting, fine wood panelling, highly decorated tiles and glass, is a popular rendezvous and one of Belfast's finest Victorian buildings (see page 117).
46 Great Victoria Street, Belfast 2. Tel: 01232–249476. Open: licensing hours.

GIANT'S RING

An intriguing circular megalithic enclosure nearly 200m in diameter, the ring has a central dolmen encircled by a high, thick bank of earth. The site, thought to be 4,000 years old, was used for horseracing – three laps to the mile (1.6km) – in the 18th century.

Near Edenderry village, south Belfast. Approach via Ballynahatty Road. Car park. Freely accessible.

GRAND OPERA HOUSE

Designed by the architect Frank Matcham and opened in 1895, this traditional Victorian theatre underwent substantial restoration and re-opened in 1980 (see page 117).
Great Victoria Street, Belfast 1. Tel: 01232–240411. Open: for performances.

LAGAN LOOKOUT CENTRE

Overlooking Belfast's River Lagan, the centre focuses on the city's social and industrial history.
Donegall Quay, Belfast 1. Tel: 01232–315444. Open: March to September, Monday to Friday 11am–5pm, Saturday noon–5pm, Sunday 2–5pm; October to February, Monday to Friday 11.30am–3.30pm, Saturday 1–4.30pm, Sunday 2–4.30pm. Admission charge.

QUEEN'S UNIVERSITY

The architectural style of the main building, designed by Sir Charles Lanyon, standing beyond a wide, grassed area, with paved cloisters and a tower entrance, has echoes of Magdalen College at Oxford University in England. Other university buildings are dotted around Stranmillis Road (see page 117).
University Road, Belfast 7.

ST ANNE'S CATHEDRAL

Building of this Anglican basilica in neo-Romanesque style began in 1899 and took about 80 years to complete. Under the floor of the unusually high nave lies the body of Lord Edward Carson, opposer of Home Rule.
Corner Donegall and York Streets, Belfast 1. Tel: 01232–328332. Donation appreciated.

SINCLAIR SEAMEN'S CHURCH

Sailors have worshipped here since 1853. Sermons are preached from a pulpit built like a ship's prow, and the organ has port and starboard navigation lights.
Corporation Square, Belfast 1. No telephone. Open: summer, Wednesday 2–4pm; services Sunday 11.30am and 7pm.

STORMONT

The former Northern Ireland Parliament building is not open to the public, but people can wander in the parklands which line the 1.5km drive.
10km east of the city, off the Newtownards road, Belfast 9. Grounds are open during daylight hours. Free.

BELFAST

ULSTER MUSEUM

Gold and silver jewellery from the *Girona*, a Spanish Armada vessel wrecked off the Giant's Causeway in 1588, can be seen among exhibits covering 9,000 years. International art, Irish furniture, glass, and countless items of interest are on display. The museum has become an important world centre for Spanish Armada studies.

Botanic Gardens, Stranmillis Road, Belfast 7. Tel: 01232–381251. Open: Monday to Friday 10am–5pm, Saturday 1–5pm, Sunday 2–5pm. Free.

CO DOWN
ANNALONG CORN MILL

This 19th-century water-powered mill, now restored to working order, has an exhibition explaining the history of flour milling. There is also a herb garden, a visitor centre, café and antiques shop.

Marine Park, Annalong. Tel: 01396– 768736. Open: June to August, daily 2–6pm; Easter to May, September and October, weekends and public holidays 2–6pm (guided tours). Admission charge.

ARK OPEN FARM

Nigerian pygmy goats, miniature horses, Jacob's sheep, rare breeds of pig and other creatures are featured at this small farm, along with a pets' corner and pony rides.

296 Bangor Road, Newtownards. Tel: 01247–812672/820445. Open: Monday to Saturday 10am–6pm, Sunday 2–6pm. Admission charge.

BALLYCOPELAND WINDMILL

This late 18th-century tower mill, which operated until 1915, is once again working. There is an electrically-run model of the mill, and a visitor centre in the miller's house.

On the B172, 1.5km west of Millisle. Tel: 01247–861413. Open: April to September, Tuesday to Saturday 10am–7pm, Sunday 2–7pm. Admission charge.

BRONTË HOMELAND INTERPRETIVE CENTRE

Drumballyroney school and church is where Patrick Brontë, father of the three literary sisters, taught and preached before moving to Yorkshire. Now preserved, the centre marks the start of a

One of several buildings reconstructed at the Ulster Folk and Transport Museum (see page 103)

Annalong's 19th-century corn mill stands
on the edge of the harbour

13km scenic drive signposted 'Brontë
Homeland', including Patrick's
birthplace at Emdale.
*Off the B10, 14km southeast of
Banbridge. Tel: 018206–31152. Open:
March to October, Tuesday to Friday
11am–5pm, weekends 2–6pm. Admission
charge.*

CASTLE WARD
Very much a His and Hers house. He
(Lord Bangor) wanted a classical
Palladian home. She (his wife, Anne)
wanted Strawberry Hill Gothic, which
was all the rage in the 1760s. As a result,
the front is classic, the back anything
but. The marriage did not last, but the
house, now a National Trust property,
survives. Buildings include a corn mill, a
saw mill, a slaughterhouse and a
Victorian laundry. There is also a
children's pastime centre.
*2.5km west of Strangford. Tel: 01396–
881204. House open: May to August,
Friday to Wednesday 1–6pm; Easter,
September and October, weekends only.
Estate: daylight hours year-round.
Admission charge.*

DOWN COUNTY MUSEUM
Housed in a former jail built in the late
18th century, this museum includes a
small display about St Patrick, Ireland's
patron saint, plus local Stone Age
artefacts and Bronze Age gold pieces.
*The Mall, Downpatrick. Tel: 01396–
615218. Open: Monday to Friday 11am–
5pm, weekends 2–5pm. Closed: Sunday
and Monday from mid-September to mid-
June. Free.*

DOWNPATRICK AND ARDGLASS
RAILWAY COMPANY
A restored 1km section of the BCDR
Downpatrick-Ardglass branch line runs
from Market Street, Downpatrick. The
steam engine *Guinness,* or one of two
diesel locomotives, hauls the train
on summer Sundays.
*Market Street, Downpatrick. Tel: 01396–
830141. Admission charge.*

EXPLORIS
Many of the creatures that thrive in the
waters of Strangford Lough can be
viewed – and some even touched – in
this sea aquarium. The Lough's
inhabitants include wolf fish and sharks
(see page 103).
*Castle Street, Portaferry. Tel: 01247–
728062. Open Monday to Saturday
10am–6pm, Sunday 1–6pm; to 5pm
September to March. Admission charge.*

HILLSBOROUGH FORT
Built in 1650, Hillsborough Fort was re-
modelled in the 18th century. Across the
road is Hillsborough Castle which was
the scene of the signing of the Anglo-
Irish agreement in 1985, and is the
former residence of the Governor of
Northern Ireland.
*Hillsborough. Tel: 01846–683285. Fort
open: April to September, Tuesday to
Saturday 10am–7pm, Sunday 2–7pm;
October to March, Tuesday to Saturday
10am–4pm, Sunday 2–4pm; grounds open
until dusk. Free.*

INCH ABBEY

This ruined Cistercian abbey, in a lovely woodland setting in the Quoile marshes, is approached by a causeway. John de Courcey founded the abbey in the 1180s on the site of a 9th-century monastery. The monks at Inch were English, having come from Furness Abbey, Lancashire. The triple east window still stands.
1.5km northwest of Downpatrick, off the A7. No telephone. Open: Easter to September, Tuesday to Saturday 10am–7pm, Sunday 2–7pm; October to March, Tuesday to Saturday 10am–4pm, Sunday 2–4pm. Admission charge.

MOUNT STEWART HOUSE AND GARDENS

The magnificent gardens, created by Lady Londonderry in the 1920s, support an enormous plant collection which enjoys the mild climate. Each garden has a theme – the Italian garden, the Spanish garden, the Shamrock garden, the Peace garden. The house (National Trust) contains antique

Tribute at the grave of Ireland's patron saint

furniture from Europe, collections of porcelain and important paintings. The Temple of the Winds is an 18th-century folly in classical Greek style, with views over Strangford Lough.
A20, 8km southeast of Newtownards. Tel: 012477–88387/88487. Open: May to September, daily 1–6pm; April and October, weekends and public holidays only. Grounds open from 10.30pm. Admission charge.

ST PATRICK'S GRAVE

St Patrick is reputed to be buried near the site of an old round tower in the churchyard at Down Cathedral, along with the bones of St Brigid and St Columba. A granite slab covers the hole made by pilgrims' feet.
Downpatrick. Freely accessible.

SAUL

St Patrick is thought to have landed near Saul and founded his first church here. From here he travelled the country converting the Irish. The 1932 St Patrick's Memorial Church was built where St Patrick's Abbey is believed to have stood.
Northeast of Downpatrick. Open: daily.

SCRABO COUNTRY PARK

Built in 1857 as a memorial to the 3rd Marquis of Londonderry, Scrabo Tower now serves as a countryside centre with woodland walks, quarries and interesting wildlife. Visitors can climb the 122 steps to the top of the 41m-high tower for outstanding views over Strangford.
Signposted from Newtownards. Tel: 01247–811491. Tower open: Easter and June to September, Saturday to Thursday, 11am–6.30pm. Free. Park: freely accessible.

Mount Stewart's Italianate-style garden is one of the most outstanding in Ireland

STRANGFORD LOUGH
One of Europe's richest places for marine wildlife, this large sea inlet, studded with 120 islands, is home to hundreds of marine animal species – from molluscs and sponges to birds and large colonies of seals.

STRUELL WELLS
Four wells reputed to have healing powers, and first recorded in 1306, are fed by an underground stream. There are men's and women's bath houses and a drinking well built around 1600. Mass is celebrated at the site at midsummer.
Off the B1, 2.5km east of Downpatrick. Freely accessible.

ULSTER FOLK AND TRANSPORT MUSEUM
Original farmhouses, cottages, watermills, a church, a school and village buildings were moved stone by stone and re-erected to form this highly acclaimed outdoor museum. Inside, the transport section ranges from donkey creels to aircraft.
Cultra, Holywood, 11km east of Belfast. Tel: 01232–428428. Open: April to June and September, Monday to Friday 9.30am–5pm, Saturday 10.30am–6pm, Sunday noon–6pm; October to March, Monday to Friday 9.30am–4pm, weekends 12.30–4.30pm. Admission charge.

CO ARMAGH
ARDRESS HOUSE
This 17th-century farmhouse has a fine 18th-century front and an elegant drawing room with superb neoclassical plasterwork. The grounds contain a cobbled farmyard with livestock, and a woodland walk – the Ladies' Mile – surrounds the estate.
On the B28 at Annaghmore, 11km west of Portadown. Tel: 01762–851236. Open: April, May and September, weekends and public holidays 2–6pm; June to August, Wednesday to Monday 2–6pm. Farmyard: May and September, Monday and Wednesday to Friday noon–4pm. Admission charge.

RELIGION

There are few countries in the western world where religion is so much a part of the everyday scene. The differences between the two Irelands are characterised by the number of Marian grottoes and shrines (Roman Catholic) in the Republic and the dour chapels and Orange Order halls (Protestant) in the North.

All over the island there are hundreds of ruined churches, many of them still playing an important role.

On both sides of the border, churches built since the 19th century tend to be stark: gaunt, steepled buildings pointing a granite-grey finger at the sky. But their huge car parks testify to the size of church-going communities.

Above: St Patrick's Church of Ireland Cathedral, Armagh
Below: a wayside shrine in honour of the Blessed Virgin Mary
Below left: march of the Orange Order

Below: inside Dublin's Catholic Pro-Cathedral

Christianity arrived in Ireland in the fourth century. The country's remoteness and difficult terrain attracted many religious refugees whose monastic communities and centres of learning established Ireland's reputation as 'a nation of saints and scholars'.

Ireland's political division and the deep religious split in the North are manifestations of 'the Troubles' which have existed for centuries. Seizure of Catholic property and successive 'plantations' of Protestant settlers from England and Scotland added fuel to the flames of rebellion.

But in everyday terms, religion today expresses itself in simple traditions: an old woman crossing herself at a shrine; mourners adding a cross to a roadside heap whenever a funeral passes at Kilmore Quay, Co Wexford. And conversation everywhere is peppered by such evocations as, 'Tis a grand day, thanks be to God.'

THE ARGORY

The Argory is a neoclassical 1820s mansion with an imposing stable yard and sundial garden in 121 hectares of wooded countryside overlooking the River Blackwater. The house contains a collection of antique furniture and an acetylene gas plant which still lights some of the rooms.

Off the B28, 11km west of Portadown. Tel: 01868–784753. Open: Easter 2–6pm; April, May and September, weekends 2–6pm; June to August, Wednesday to Monday 2–6pm. Public holidays from 1pm. Admission charge.

The Sundial Garden at The Argory

ARMAGH FRIARY

Set in the grounds of the Archbishop's Palace are the ruins of the longest friary in Ireland, founded for the Franciscans in 1263 by Archbishop Patrick O'Scanail. The **Palace Stables Heritage Centre** portrays typical daily life in the Archbishop's Palace in 1776. There are working stables, a smithy, craft demonstrations and exhibitions.

Friary Road, Armagh. Tel: 01861–529629. Friary: freely accessible. Heritage Centre: April to September, Monday to Saturday 10am–6pm, Sunday 1–6pm; October to March, Monday to Saturday 10am–5pm, Sunday 2–5pm (admission charge).

ARMAGH PLANETARIUM

Visitors can experience space travel through the latest hands-on computer exhibits in the planetarium's Hall of Astronomy. The planetarium theatre has a worldwide reputation for its innovative 'star shows' (booking advised). On display are astronomical instruments.

College Hill, Armagh. Tel: 01861–523689. Open: Monday to Friday 11.30am–5pm, weekends 1.30–5pm. Shows – daily 3pm, also 2pm weekends. Admission charge.

GOSFORD FOREST PARK

Several of the walks through the former demesne of Gosford Castle, in early 19th-century mock-Norman style, were devised by Jonathan Swift, author of *Gulliver's Travels*. Traditional breeds of poultry strut in open paddocks, and ornamental pigeons coo in a dovecote. The estate also includes a deer park, walled garden and nature trail.

Gosford Road, Markethill. Tel: 01861–551277. Castle: not open to the public. Park open: daily 10am–dusk. Admission charge.

KILLEVY CHURCHES

Joined together by a common gable, these two churches, one 11th-century, the other 15th-century, are on the site of a nunnery which survived from the 5th century until the Dissolution in 1542. Its founder, St Monenna (also known as St Blinne) is believed to be buried under a granite slab in the graveyard.

Signposted off the B113, 6km southwest of Newry. Freely accessible.

LOUGH NEAGH DISCOVERY CENTRE

This centre on Oxford Island has a wildlife exhibition and there are boat trips, and talks on the flora and fauna of the Lough Neagh basin. Oxford Island is

a birdwatcher's paradise with more than 8km of walks and viewing hides.
Oxford Island, exit 10 from the M1. Tel: 01762–322205. Open: April to September, daily 10am–7pm; October to March, Wednesday to Sunday 10am–5pm. Admission charge.

NAVAN CENTRE

The history and legends of the great Iron Age hill fort which was the ancient capital of the Kings of Ulster are told with the aid of computer technology.
On the A28, 1.5km west of Armagh. Tel: 01861–525550. Open: Fort – freely accessible. Visitor centre – April to June and September, Monday to Friday 10am–6pm, Saturday 11am–6pm, Sunday noon–6pm; July and August, Monday to Saturday 10am–7pm, Sunday 11am–7pm; October to March, Monday to Friday 10am–5pm, Saturday 11am–5pm, Sunday noon–5pm. Admission charge.

Computerised exhibits at Armagh's Planetarium

PEATLANDS PARK

This park tells the story of peat boglands over a period of 10,000 years. There are areas of cutaway bogland, virgin bogs, small lakes and low wooded hills. A narrow-gauge railway, originally used for carrying turf, takes visitors out on to the bog to prevent erosion.
Exit 13 from the M1, 11km east of Dungannon, Co Tyrone. Tel: 01762–851102. Open: daily 9am–dusk. Visitor centre – Easter to May and September, weekends and public holidays 2–6pm; June to August, daily 2–6pm. Charge for railway.

ROYAL IRISH FUSILIERS MUSEUM

This museum relates the regiment's history from 1793 to 1968. Exhibits include a soldier's uniform from the Peninsular War and a 1943 Christmas card from Adolf Hitler.
Sovereign's House, The Mall, Armagh. Tel: 01861–522911. Open: Monday to Friday 10am–12.30pm, 1.30–4.30pm. Admission charge.

ST PATRICK'S TRIAN

Two attractions in one are presented at this interpretive centre. 'The Armagh Story' traces developments from prehistoric times to the present day, and features St Patrick, who built a church here in the 5th century. The other attraction, of particular interest to children, celebrates 'The Land of Lilliput', based on Dean Swift's *Gulliver's Travels*. There is also a restaurant.

40 English Street, Armagh. Tel: 01861–521801. Open: April to September, Monday to Saturday 10am–6pm, Sunday 1–6pm; October to March, Monday to Saturday 10am–5pm, Sunday 2–5pm. Admission charge.

CO MONAGHAN
COUNTY MUSEUM

Monaghan's county museum, housed in an 18th-century market house in the country town, is an award-winning museum with exhibits representing 200 years of local history, while pride of place goes to the 600-year-old bronze processional Cross of Clogher.

Hill Street, Monaghan. Tel: 047–82928. Open: Tuesday to Saturday 11am–5pm. Closed: October to May from 1–2pm. Free.

CO CAVAN
CARRAIG CRAFT VISITORS' CENTRE

Rod and rush basketwork in the form of hats, creels, bread baskets, shopping baskets and other items are displayed. The basketry museum has an audio-visual presentation and there are demonstrations, lectures and craft workshops.

Mountnugent. Tel: 049–40179. Open: Monday to Saturday 10am–6pm, Sunday 2–6pm. Admission charge.

CAVAN COUNTY MUSEUM

The former convent of the Sisters of Poor Clare, this new museum traces the history of the county from pre-Christian times to the present day.

Virginia Road, Ballyjamesduff. Tel: 049–44070. Open: Tuesday to Saturday 10am–5pm. Free (charge for exhibitions).

CO FERMANAGH
BELLEEK POTTERY

Ireland's oldest pottery reveals the skills that produce its fine china and distinctive basketware. There are factory tours and visitors can take their time browsing in the museum, visitors' centre

Belleek is famed for its parian china

The Georgian splendour of Florence Court, in the grounds of its beautiful estate (see page 110)

and shop. The restaurant serves refreshment on fine Belleek table-ware (see page 121).

Belleek. Tel: 013656–58501. Visitor centre open: March to June and September, Monday to Friday 9am–6pm, Saturday 10am–6pm, Sunday 2–6pm; October to February, Monday to Friday 9am–5.30pm, Saturday 10am–6pm, Sunday 11am–8pm. Tours: Monday to Thursday 9.30am–4.15pm, Friday 9.30am–3.15pm. Admission charge

CASTLE ARCHDALE COUNTRY PARK

On the shores of Lower Lough Erne, the park has something for everyone – picnic areas, walks, open-air exhibits of natural history and agricultural machinery and an exhibition featuring the Battle of the Atlantic during World War II. Pony trekking, boat rental and cycle hire are available. There is a ruined castle in the surrounding woodlands and the marina has concrete jetties and slipways built for wartime flying boats (see page 121).

Off the B82, 5km south of Kesh. Tel: 013656–21588. Freely accessible.

CASTLE COOLE

The stateliest of the National Trust's stately homes in Northern Ireland, Castle Coole was completed in 1798. It was designed by James Wyatt and built for the Earls of Belmore. The house has an imposing Palladian front and there are fine furnishings and plasterwork within.

On the A4, 1.5km southeast of Enniskillen. Tel: 01365–322690. Open: Easter, April and September, weekends 1–6pm; May to August, Friday to Wednesday 1–6pm. Admission charge (grounds freely accessible).

DEVENISH ISLAND

The island has extensive monastic ruins and probably Ireland's most perfect round tower. The earliest ruins and the tower are 12th-century, but the monastery was founded by St Molaise, (died 563), and remained an important religious centre until the 17th century.

By ferry from Trory Point, 5km north of Enniskillen, junction of the A32 and B82. Round tower and museum open: April to September, Tuesday to Saturday 10am–7pm, Sunday 2–7pm. Admission charge.

Glass maker at Tyrone Crystal, famous for its fine cut glass

FLORENCE COURT

One of Ulster's most important 18th-century houses, Florence Court was built by the Earls of Enniskillen. The house is noted for its extravagant rococo plasterwork and fine furniture. The surrounding forest park contains an ancient Irish yew tree, said to be the mother of all Irish yews (see page 121).
13km southwest of Enniskillen via the A4 and A32. Tel: 01365–348249. Open: Easter, April and September, weekends 1–6pm; May to August, Wednesday to Monday, 1–6pm. Admission charge.

LOUGH NAVAR FOREST

Red deer and wild goats roam the forest, and a steep zigzag path, part of the Ulster Way, leads to one of the best panoramas in Ireland, with views across Lough Erne and to counties Donegal and Sligo.

Signposted off the A46, 8km northwest of Derrygonnelly. Tel: 013656–41256. Open: daily 10am–dusk. Admission charge.

MARBLE ARCH CAVES

One of Europe's finest cave systems can be toured by electric boat and on foot in a 90-minute guided exploration of underground rivers, waterfalls, winding passages and huge chambers with impressive stalagmite and stalactite formations. Over 300 million years of history is here in among a strange landscape of chasms and valleys. Take comfortable shoes and a sweater as it can get quite chilly. The visitor centre has an exhibition area, an audio-visual theatre and restaurant (see page 121).
19km southwest of Enniskillen, following the A4 (Sligo road) and the A32, near Florence Court. Tel: 01365–348855. Open: mid-March to September, daily 10.30am–4.30pm (weather permitting). Admission charge.

REGIMENTAL MUSEUM OF THE ROYAL INNISKILLING FUSILIERS

Brightly coloured uniforms, arms and colours outline the story of this famous regiment, housed in the medieval castle of Enniskillen, seat of the Maguires. Exhibits include Napoleonic battle trophies, badges and medals, musical instruments and the bugle that sounded the charge at the Battle of the Somme in 1916 (see page 120). Also housed in the castle is the **Fermanagh County Museum**, with displays on the landscape and people of Fermanagh.
Castle Keep, Castle Barracks, Enniskillen. Tel: 01365–325000. Open: Tuesday to Friday 10am–5pm, Saturday and Monday 2–5pm, Sunday (July and August) 2–5pm. Closed weekends October to April. Admission charge.

CO TYRONE

ALTMORE OPEN FARM

Visitors can learn the history of the Sperrin Mountains regions and see rare breeds of farm animals and poultry on this 71-hectare sheep farm. There is pony trekking in summer, and fishing.
32 Altmore Road, Pomeroy. Tel: 01868–758977. Open: daily 9am–dusk. Admission charge.

ARDBOE CROSS

On the west shore of Lough Neagh is one of Ireland's finest northern high crosses, marking the site of a monastery. Over 5m high, this 10th-century cross has Old and New Testament scenes carved on either side.
Lough Neagh, east of Cookstown, off the B73. Freely accessible.

BEAGHMORE STONE CIRCLES

Beaghmore is a remarkable prehistoric site, unlike any other in Ireland. Consisting of seven Bronze Age stone circles in a complex ceremonial area, discovered beneath a layer of peat, its origins and purpose are unknown.
Signposted from the A505 between Cookstown and Gortin. Freely accessible.

GRANT ANCESTRAL HOUSE

John Simpson, great-grandfather of Ulysses S Grant, 18th President of the United States, was born at Ballygawley in 1738 and emigrated to Pennsylvania in 1760. The two-room thatched farmhouse where he lived has been restored, and the adjoining visitor centre has an audio-visual theatre and exhibits of rural life.
Dergina, Ballygawley. Tel: 016625–57133. Open: April to September, Monday to Saturday noon–5pm, Sunday 2–6pm. Admission charge.

TYRONE CRYSTAL

Visitors can tour the factory and watch the various stages – blowing, marking, cutting and finishing – in the production of fine glassware.
Killybrackey, Coalisland Road, Dungannon. Tel: 018687–25335. Tours: Monday to Thursday 9.30am–3.30pm, Friday 9.30am–noon, Saturday 9.30am–3pm. Craft centre open: Monday to Saturday 9.30am–5pm. Admission charge.

ULSTER-AMERICAN FOLK PARK

This open-air museum traces the connections of famous Americans with their Ulster ancestry, from Davy Crockett to an Archbishop of New York, including a handful of US Presidents. The hard facts of 19th-century emigration are graphically demonstrated in the Ship and Dockside Gallery, where the smells and sounds of an overcrowded emigrant ship are reproduced.
Castletown, 5km north of Omagh, on the A5. Tel: 01662–243292. Open: Easter to September, Monday to Saturday 11am–6.30pm, Sunday and public holidays 11.30am–7pm; October to Easter, Monday to Friday 10.30am–5pm. Last admission 90 minutes before closing. Admission charge.

ULSTER HISTORY PARK

The human history of Ulster, from the arrival of primitive settlers in 8000BC to the end of the 17th century is presented, with reconstructions of Stone Age houses and round towers.
Cullion, 11km north of Omagh, on the B48. Tel: 016626–48188. Open: April to September, Monday to Saturday 10.30am–6.30pm, Sunday 11.30am–7pm, public holidays 10.30am–7pm; October to March, Monday to Friday 10.30am–5pm. Last admission 90 minutes before closing.

WELLBROOK BEETLING MILL

An 18th-century water-powered mill, restored to working order by the National Trust, demonstrates beetling – the final process in which linen is hammered to give it its characteristic sheen.

Off the A505, 6.5km west of Cookstown. Tel: 016487–51735. Open: April to June and September, weekends and public holidays 2–6pm; July to August, Wednesday to Monday, 2–6pm. Admission charge.

WILSON ANCESTRAL HOME

This simple thatched, whitewashed house in the Sperrin Mountains was the home of the grandfather of the 28th US President, Woodrow Wilson. It still contains some original furniture.

Dergalt, Strabane. Tel: 01662–243292 for details. Admission charge.

Traditional methods are still used to produce fine pottery in Donegal

CO DONEGAL

DONEGAL CASTLE

Close to the town centre, this fortified manor house dates from the 15th century, but underwent much re-building in the early 17th century, when it was incorporated into a Jacobean structure by Sir Basil Brooke.

Tirchonaill Street, Donegal. Tel: 073– 22405. Open: 10am–6.30pm. Admission charge.

DONEGAL COUNTY MUSEUM

Artefacts dating from the Stone Age to the Donegal Railway era are exhibited.

High Road, Letterkenny. Tel: 074–24613. Open: Monday to Friday 10am–4.30pm, Saturday 1–4.30pm. Free.

DONEGAL PARIAN CHINA

Short 15-minute tours of the factory give the visitor an insight into the traditional methods used to produce this delicate china and porcelain. There is also the chance to buy products at factory prices. The guided tours run from Monday to Friday.

Ballyshannon. Tel: 072–51826. Open: March to September, Monday to Saturday 9am–5.30pm, Sunday 10.30am–4.30pm; October to December, Monday to Friday 9am–5.30pm.

ERRIGAL MOUNTAIN

Errigal is Donegal's highest peak at 750m. Those who know say it is an easy climb; others say scrabbling on the loose scree and the near-perpendicular topmost peak can be daunting. All agree the view from the summit is supreme.

Dunlewey. Freely accessible.

GLEBE GALLERY

The Glebe Gallery houses the art collection of Derek Hill, landscape and portrait painter, who worked here until

Glebe House contains Derek Hill's extensive art collection, which he presented to the nation

1954. He presented the house and collection, which includes works by Picasso and Renoir, to the nation in 1981.
On the shores of Garton Lough, by Glenveagh Park. Tel: 074–37071. Open: Easter week and mid-May to September, Saturday to Thursday 11am–6.30pm. Admission charge.

GLENCOLUMBKILLE FOLK VILLAGE

The Folk Village features a group of three traditional-style cottages spanning three centuries, each furnished according to the period it represents (1720s, 1820s and 1920s).
Glencolumbkille. Tel: 073–30017. Open: Easter to September, Monday to Saturday 10am–6pm, Sunday noon–6pm. Admission charge.

GLENVEAGH NATIONAL PARK AND CASTLE

Glenveagh is one of the last places in Ireland to be influenced by man. The visitor centre introduces the 9,600-hectare park's natural history – mountain moorland, lakes and wood-land. The dramatically-sited castle here is set in glorious gardens. There are nature trails, and one of Ireland's last two herds of red deer live in the park.
Church Hill, Letterkenny. Tel: 074–37088/ 37262. Open: Easter to October, daily 10.30am–6.30pm (to 7.30pm Sunday, June to August). Closed: Monday in April and October and Friday in October.

IONAD COIS LOCHA

Carding, spinning and weaving demonstrations, story-telling, boat trips, an adventure play area, farm tours and craft shop feature in this award-winning lakeside centre where Irish is spoken.
Dunlewey, Letterkenny. Tel: 075–31699. Open: mid-March to early April, Saturday 10.30am–6pm, Sunday 11am–7pm; early April to early November, Monday to Saturday 10.30am–6pm, Sunday 11am–7pm. Admission charge.

TULLYARVAN MILL CULTURAL AND EXHIBITION CENTRE

Converted from a 19th-century corn mill, this visitor centre has a textile museum, wildlife display, art workshop, craft shop and coffee shop.
Buncrana, Inishowen. Tel: 077–61613. Open: June to September, Monday to Saturday 10am–6pm, Sunday 2–6pm. Admission charge.

CO LONDONDERRY

FOYLE VALLEY RAILWAY CENTRE

The centre outlines the region's railway history, featuring the narrow-gauge systems of the Co Donegal Railway and Londonderry & Lough Swilly Railway.
Foyle Road, Derry. Tel: 01504–265234. Open: May to September, Tuesday to Saturday 10am–5pm, Sunday 2–6pm; May to September, train rides Saturday and Sunday afternoon. Phone for out-of-season opening times. Admission charge.

ROE VALLEY COUNTRY PARK

Ulster's first domestic hydroelectric power station, opened in 1896, is on show here, and much of its original equipment is preserved, together with old water mills for linen production.
Off the B192, 1.5km south of Limavady. Tel: 01504–722074. Open: visitor centre – daily 10am–5pm (to 4pm October to Easter); park – freely accessible. Free.

ST COLUMB'S CATHEDRAL

Scenes from the great siege of Derry (1688–9) are depicted in stained glass. An audio-visual show relates the siege and outlines the cathedral's history.
Bishop Street Within, Derry. Tel: 01504–267313. Open: Monday to Saturday 9am–5pm (to 4pm November to March). Admission charge.

CO ANTRIM

ANDREW JACKSON CENTRE

The parents of the seventh US President emigrated from Carrickfergus in 1765. This 18th-century thatched cottage stands on the site of their original home, and has living quarters, store rooms and stables all under one roof. Graphic displays and a video cover the background to the Ulster-American emigration.
Boneybefore, Carrickfergus. Tel: 01960–366455. Open: April to October, Monday to Friday 10am–1pm, 2–4pm, weekends 2–4pm; open to 6pm June to September. Admission charge.

CARRICKFERGUS CASTLE

Northern Ireland's largest, best preserved Norman castle was begun by John de Courcy in 1180. Displays feature life in the castle throughout its history.

Historical figures haunt Carrickfergus Castle

St Columb's Stone, Derry

Information panels have been set up along four marked walks to help visitors interpret the astonishing formations. The National Trust visitor centre has fascinating displays of the region's geology, flora and fauna, and local history exhibits.

Port-na-Spaniagh, a short walk east of the Causeway, is the site of the wrecked Spanish Armada treasure ship *Girona*.

Causeway Head, 3km north of Bushmills on the B146. Tel: 012657–31159 (31855 – visitor centre). Causeway freely accessible (minibus with wheelchair access runs from the visitor centre daily, 17 March to end October). Centre open: July to August, daily 10am–7pm (earlier closing rest of year). Admission charge for car park and audio-visual show.

Carrickfergus. Tel: 01960–351273. Open: April to September, Monday to Saturday 10am–6pm, Sunday 2–6pm; October to March, Monday to Saturday 10am–4pm, Sunday 2–4pm. Last admission 30 minutes before closing. Admission charge.

CAUSEWAY SAFARI PARK

The safari park is the home of free-roaming lions and other exotic wildlife. Attractions include a farmyard area, mini-zoo and amusement park.

Leslie Hill Heritage Farm Park can be found 16km from the safari park.

28 Benvarden Road (B67), Ballymoney. Tel: 012657–41474. Open: April, May and September, weekends 10.30am–6.30pm; June to August, daily 10.30am–6.30pm. Admission charge.

GIANT'S CAUSEWAY AND CENTRE

A World Heritage Site, the Causeway consists of 40,000 hexagonal basalt columns – an incredible freak of nature.

KNIGHT RIDE AND HERITAGE PLAZA

Monorail cars take visitors on a tour of 1,000 years of Carrickfergus history.

Antrim Street, Carrickfergus. Tel: 01960–366455. Open: April to September, Monday to Saturday 10am–6pm, Sunday noon–6pm; October to March, Monday to Saturday 10am–5pm, Sunday noon–5pm. Last admission 30 minutes before closing. Admission charge.

OLD BUSHMILLS DISTILLERY

Established in 1608, Bushmills is the world's oldest licensed distillery. Visitors are taken on a one-hour guided tour to see how the famous whiskey is produced – and are rewarded with a tot.

Distillery Road, Bushmills. Tel: 012657–31521 (ask for tours department). Open: Monday to Thursday 9am–noon, 1.30–3.30pm, Friday 9–11.45am (to 3pm July to September), Saturday 10am–3pm. Admission charge.

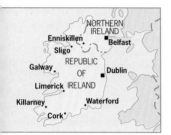

Belfast's Golden Mile

The area between Donegall Square and Shaftesbury Square is known as the Golden Mile, but it covers less than half a mile (0.8km) and the adjective owes more to commercial success than appearance. Nevertheless, this is a lively part of the city, full of interest. *Allow 1½ hours.*

Start at Donegall Square.

1 DONEGALL SQUARE

Nearby

5 Royal Belfast Academic Institution

The eastern and western sides of the square form the terminus for city buses. The square itself is dominated by the massive City Hall (see page 97), and surrounded by the statues of civic worthies, including Sir Edward Harland, founder of the shipyard, Harland and Wolff. Queen Victoria gazes haughtily towards Donegall Place. Number 17 Donegall Square North is the Linenhall Library, formerly a linen warehouse – note the carved linen drapery across the porch. The Scottish Provident Building in Donegall Square West, another huge edifice, is decorated with looms, ships, spinning wheels and ropes, symbols of Belfast's traditional industries. Yorkshire House, at No 10 Donegall Square South, features the carved heads of Homer, Shakespeare, Schiller, Michaelangelo and George Washington. *At the square's southwest corner follow Bedford Street.*

2 BEDFORD STREET

In the 19th century this was the centre of the city's linen industry and the street was dominated by warehouses. Most have now disappeared. Among the survivors are the palatial Ewart Buildings (Nos 7–17) and the Venetian-

Built in classical style, City Hall's dome has echoes of St Paul's Cathedral, London

style Bryson House at No 28. Ulster Hall, opened in 1861, was intended for grand social occasions but became a focal point for 19th-century political rallies addressed by the likes of Lloyd George and Charles Stewart Parnell. At the end of the street is the BBC Building and a fountain erected as a memorial to a 19th-century physician who died after tireless service at the Home for Incurables.
Bear right into Dublin Road.

3 DUBLIN ROAD
Dublin Road begins with an abundance of furniture shops and furnishing companies, and ends with shops selling second-hand books, stamps and prints. At No 49, opposite the Salvation Army's public relations department, is The Elbow, a popular pub with a plush, intimate atmosphere.
Continue into Shaftesbury Square.

4 SHAFTESBURY SQUARE
Shaftesbury Square marks the beginning of Belfast's student quarter – Queen's University (see page 98) is near by – with lots of small shops and good eating places. Formed by the conjunction of six major thoroughfares, it is Belfast's equivalent of Piccadilly Circus or Times Square. The two supine figures

decorating the façade of the Ulster Bank are known locally as 'Draft' and 'Overdraft'. Next to the post office, on the east side, is Donegall Pass, one of six wide avenues laid across the 17th-century estate of the third Earl of Donegall.
From the west side of Shaftesbury Square walk north along Great Victoria Street.

5 GREAT VICTORIA STREET
Once fashionably residential, this is now a commercial thoroughfare undergoing re-development. It consists mainly of record shops, second-hand book stores, charity shops and ethnic restaurants. Its stars, however, are the Crown Liquor Saloon and the Grand Opera House, the first opposite and the second alongside the Europa Hotel. Built around 1885, the Crown is a wild extravagance of brilliant tiles, stained glass and panelled snugs – all intimately lit by gas lamps and restored by the National Trust (see page 98).
The Grand Opera House, another recent restoration, was opened in 1895 and now presents a wide-ranging programme (see page 98).
Continue into Fisherwick Place, then College Square East, turning right into Wellington Place to complete the walk back at Donegall Square North.

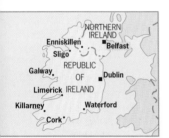

Belfast's Shopping Area

The city centre north of Donegall Square is Belfast's major shopping precinct, with many large stores and shopping malls. Largely pedestrianised for security reasons, it has some fascinating side streets and secretive, though not threatening, alleys. *Allow 1½ hours.*

Begin at Donegall Square North and proceed northwards along Donegall Place.

Nearby

1 Linen Hall Library

1 City Hall (see page 97)

1 DONEGALL PLACE

Belfast's Victorian prosperity is reflected in the solid, ornate architecture of the office buildings and stores in Donegall

Place. Notable examples are the pink sandstone Marks & Spencer building, a linen warehouse when it was erected in 1869; and the copper domes of the former Robinson and Cleaver store, with a carved façade featuring some of the company's distinguished customers.
Turn right into Castle Lane.

2 CASTLE LANE

Halfway along this pleasantly pedestrianised lane, on the right, is Callender Street, the main depot for pressing, weighing and packing linen in the late 18th century. Callendering is the smoothing process that gives bleached linen its final sheen.
Continue to Arthur Square.

3 ARTHUR SQUARE

The city's oldest square is named after Sir Arthur Chichester, the Elizabethan adventurer who received Belfast as a reward in 1603 for defeating the great Hugh O'Neill. With its bandstand, clock and buskers, the square today is a relaxing spot for shoppers.
Cross the square directly and enter Ann Street.

4 ANN STREET

Ann Street allows a glimpse of 19th-century Belfast, when half the city's streets were small courts and 'entries' – narrow alleyways. Half a dozen of these can be seen on the left. Joy's Entry carries the name of the family that published Britain's first daily newspaper, the *Belfast News Letter,* in 1737.
Turn left into Pottinger's Entry.

5 POTTINGER'S ENTRY

This was a fashionable address in the 1820s when the entry had 34 houses. Today it contains one of Belfast's classical saloon bars, the Morning Star, with its frosted-glass windows and polished interior of mahogany and brass.
Turn right into High Street.

6 HIGH STREET

On the corner of High Street and Victoria Street is the imposing Protestant church of St George's, completed in 1816. Its splendid portico came from a palatial house that was intended as a home for Frederick Hervey, Earl Bishop of Derry, but when he died the house was dismantled and the portico moved to St George's. The nearby Albert Memorial Clock Tower tilts some 1.3m from the vertical as a result of poor foundations. The tower was erected in 1865 and the tilt was noticed as long ago as 1901.
Cross Victoria Street to Queen's Square and on to Donegall Quay.

7 DONEGALL QUAY

The large yellow Italianate building overlooking the river is Custom House, built between 1854 and 1857 by Sir Charles Lanyon, architect of many of Belfast's Victorian buildings. Near by a recently constructed weir across the River Lagan can be viewed from the Lagan Lookout Centre (see page 98).
From Donegall Quay turn left into Albert Square and continue into Waring Street. Cross Bridge Street to Rosemary Street and turn left into Wine Cellar Entry.

8 WINE CELLAR ENTRY

Here is the city's oldest pub, White's Tavern, opened in 1630 and re-built in 1790. An open fire and plush seating contribute to a welcoming atmosphere.
Continue to High Street, turning right into Castle Place. At Donegall Place turn left to return to the walk's starting point.

Fermanagh Lakeland

Fermanagh is an area of stunning beauty, with lakes and mountains, mysterious islands and enigmatic hints at a pagan past. *Allow 1 day.*

Begin at Enniskillen

1 ENNISKILLEN

Nearby

4 Lough Navar Forest (see page 110)

Enniskillen straddles the River Erne which connects Upper and Lower Lough Erne. Watergate, part of the old castle, now houses the Fermanagh County Museum and the Regimental Museum of the Royal Inniskilling Fusiliers (see page 110).

Oscar Wilde and Samuel Beckett were both old boys of Portora Royal School.

From the village of Trory, 3km north of Enniskillen, a ferry runs across to Devenish Island (see page 109).
Take the A32 for 3km, then the B82 for 11km, turning off to Castle Archdale.

2 CASTLE ARCHDALE

The marina, caravan site and youth hostel can make this a busy place, but tranquillity can be found in the surrounding country park. The estate has a butterfly park, an arboretum and rare breeds of farm animals. The ruins of an old castle, razed in 1689, can be seen in the forest (see page 109).

White Island, with strange stone figures in a ruined church, can be reached by boat from Castle Archdale.
Turn left on the B82 and after 3km leave the B road and follow the scenic route for 6km to Kesh, then turn left on to the A35 for 1.5km before taking the A47 for 13km to Boa Island.

3 BOA ISLAND

Towards the far end of the island, watch for a sign to Caldragh Graveyard on the left. Park at the roadside and prepare for a possibly muddy walk of about 1km. At the end of the concrete track an overgrown old graveyard contains two uncanny stone figures among its unkempt tombstones. A double-faced Janus is smiling on one side, scowling on the other, while beside him a small hunched figure leers disconcertingly. Both figures evoke uneasy echoes of pre-Christian Ireland.
Continue on the A47 for 16km to Belleek.

4 BELLEEK

A border village, Belleek is famed for its fine basketwork china (see pages 108–9).

Take the A46 for Enniskillen and after 33km turn right and follow the signs to Monea.

5 MONEA

Monea is a ruined 17th-century castle, built by 'planters' from Scotland. It was captured by the Irish in 1641 and abandoned in 1750. An ancient *crannog* – artificial island dwelling – can be traced in the marsh in front of Monea.
Turn left leaving Monea, then left again for Enniskillen. Turn right, following signs for Boho for 8km, then turn right for Belcoo.

6 BELCOO

Noted for its first-class coarse fishing, Belcoo sits between Upper and Lower Lough Macnean. Just north of the village is the Holywell, a shrine for pilgrims.
Cross into the Republic at Blacklion for a short distance, then cross back into Northern Ireland. Follow the south shore of Lower Lough Macnean. Turn right along Marlbank Scenic Loop and drive for 5km to Marble Arch.

7 MARBLE ARCH CAVES

Electric boats take visitors on a tour of this spectacular underground system of caverns and chasms. There is an excellent visitor centre and the surrounding countryside is beautiful (see page 110).
Turn left, then right, and drive for 6km to Florence Court.

8 FLORENCE COURT

A grand Anglo-Irish mansion, Florence Court was built in the mid-18th century and named in honour of a new English wife (see page 110).
Return to Enniskillen by the A32 and the A4.

Legends and the Little People

*A*ll over Ireland you can see farm gates standing between sturdy stone posts with conical caps. The gateposts are this shape (would you believe it?) to discourage the Little People from sitting about on them for too long. At the same time, nobody wants to offend them by disturbing a mound in a field, where they are believed to live. Dreadful disaster could follow.

The hawthorn or Fairy Tree, should never be interfered with, either. Bad luck will result, probably in the form of sickness affecting livestock.

Ireland is steeped in superstition and folklore, handed down through the generations. The Banshee is greatly

The legendary Children of Lîr – condemned to live their lives as swans

feared. Some families, it seems, are haunted by this fairy, which wails and keens when a death is imminent.

Leprechauns – little men in green tunics – are reputed to sit under trees mending fairies' shoes. Leprechauns (the *Oxford Dictionary* calls them 'pygmy sprites') are said to possess a crock of gold. Any mortal who can stare at a Leprechaun gets the crock, but if his gaze wavers for an instant, the treasure disappears.

One of the best-known legends concerns the four children of Lîr, whose jealous stepmother had them turned into swans for 400 years. The sentence is now long passed, and the four died as ancient humans, but to this day it is illegal to kill swans.

Tales are told of legendary heroes like Cuchulain, The Hound of Ulster, who fought off an invading army single-handed with his javelin.

The lucky Irish shamrock turns up wherever St Patrick's Day is celebrated throughout the world. St Patrick used it to illustrate the story of the Holy Trinity.

In a land of legend and superstition it is fitting that University College, Dublin, should have a Department of Folklore, where a huge collection of documents, pictures and tapes records every aspect of the subject.

GETTING AWAY FROM IT ALL

'O Ireland, isn't it grand you look –
Like a bride in her rich adornin'?
And with all the pent-up love of my heart
I bid you top o' the mornin'!'

JOHN LOCKE, 1847–89

BEACHES

Most people who know Ireland well will argue that simply being there is getting away from it all. Generally, there is such a laid-back atmosphere about the country that few visitors shoulder the burden of care for long. Those seeking solitude may have to travel a little further than the rest, for the Irish are a gregarious people – but quiet places there are in abundance.

There is no shortage of beaches along Ireland's shoreline. Many are as beautiful as you will find anywhere in the world, ranging from long stretches of deserted dunes to intimate rocky coves.

LEINSTER

Close to Dublin, on the DART system, Dalkey and Killiney (pronounced 'Dorkee' and 'Kill-aye-nee') are attractive spots for a half-day's outing. Dalkey has narrow streets and elegant

houses. Boat trips can be taken during the summer to Dalkey Island, which has a bird sanctuary and a Martello tower. Killiney, set in a sweeping bay with neat villas, lush gardens and two Sugarloaf mountains, is often compared with the Bay of Naples.

Courtown, Co Wexford, is a pleasant harbour village 40km north of Wexford Town. Its 3km-long sandy beach, amusements and golf course make it a popular family resort. Also in Co Wexford, Kilmore Quay, about 19km southwest of Rosslare, is a pretty fishing village with excellent beaches.

MUNSTER

Ardmore, Co Cork, is a charming resort with a good beach at the base of a cliff. About 21km southwest of Dungarvan, it has impressive monastic ruins surrounding an almost intact round tower.

Birdwatchers will be attracted to Castlegregory, Co Kerry, on the western shore of Tralee Bay. The beaches are superb, and many unusual species – including Bewick's swans – have been logged at the nearby Lough Gill bird sanctuary.

Dunmore East, Co Waterford, is a delightful village of thatched cottages and friendly pubs overlooking a picturesque bay and fishing harbour 16km south of Waterford. Its sandy beaches are protected by rose-hued cliffs.

Lahinch is the busiest resort in Co Clare, but there is still plenty of room along its splendid beach and nearby dunes. The surfing is good and there is a championship golf course.

Courtown Bay, a popular family resort with its superb 3km stretch of sand

Ireland's beaches are as beautiful and varied as any you will find in the world. This one is at Dingle

CONNACHT

Some 100km northwest of Galway City, Roundstone is a relaxing, pretty village resort on the edge of a bay, and has become a popular summer resort. First settled by Scottish fishermen in the 19th century, today it has a community of artists and crafts folk whose workshops may be visited.

Spiddall, 19km west of Galway, has a well-named beach in the Silver Strand. There is good shore fishing, and in the summer there are exciting races between *currachs,* the traditional canvas-skinned boats.

Eight kilometres west of Sligo, Strandhill is a favoured place for surfing championships. For those who prefer quieter waters, Culleenamore, round the corner in Ballysadare Bay, is the place.

ULSTER

Standing on a beautiful beach on Lough Swilly, Rathmullen in Co Donegal has a ruined 16th-century priory and an informative heritage centre. It is also the start of the Fanad Drive, with even more wonderful beaches, as well as streams, lakes and mountains.

Cushendun, Co Antrim, was built in the style of a Cornish village – a tribute by Lord Cushendun to his Cornish wife. There is a good beach, and from nearby Torr Head you can see Scotland's Mull of Kintyre.

Newcastle, Co Down, is where 'the Mountains of Mourne sweep down to the sea'. A traditional and popular resort, it has a magnificent sandy beach. Towering 852m above the town is Slieve Donard.

Dun Aengus prehistoric fort perches on a cliff 90m above the sea on Inishmore

ISLANDS

Storm-battered or bathed in sunshine, obscured by mist or magnified in the strange light of a rainbow sky, the islands of Ireland beckon with a promise of rugged freedom.

Most of the islands lie within 8km of the mainland and none is more than 16km out. Each has been inhabited at some time – the wildest by no more than a hermit monk or two in the early days of Christianity. Celtic crosses, ruined chapels and dwellings are everywhere. A few are still inhabited.

Facilities are few, but the islanders extend a warm hospitality to visitors. There are a few family-run hotels and guesthouses.

THE NORTH

Five kilometres off the coast of Donegal, **Aran Island** is served by a ferry from Burtonport. The island is hilly, with rough moorland and cliffs on the Atlantic side, and sandy beaches and rock pools facing the mainland. Seven pubs and a hotel set the pace of the island's social life.

Rathlin, off the north coast of Co Antrim, is home to 30 families, mostly involved in raising sheep and cattle. Settled originally by early Christian monks, Rathlin has suffered plunder, piracy and massacre. The cave in which Robert the Bruce studied a resolute spider can be visited in good weather. The island has a bird sanctuary, a diving centre, three lighthouses and a pub. The crossing from Ballycastle takes about 50 minutes.

THE WEST

The three **Aran Islands** – Inishmore, Inishmaan and Inisheer – dominate the horizon off the coasts of Clare and Galway. Like The Burren, the islands consist mainly of bare, grey limestone scoured by Ice Age glaciers. But the bleakness is tempered by stone-walled pastures and wild flowers.

Inishmore, the largest, has 14 small villages and a fishing harbour at Kilronan. Dun Aengus is the largest of several prehistoric forts and there are many early Christian churches, including 7th-century St Benan's.

Inishmaan has two impressive prehistoric forts and the cottage in which the writer J M Synge lived.

Inisheer, southernmost of the islands, has narrow roads and a gleaming white beach on which *currachs* are built.

Rising to a height of some 500m in Clew Bay, Co Mayo, **Clare Island** will appeal to walkers. It also offers fishing, sailboarding, pony trekking and diving. Clare's wildlife includes dolphins, seals and otters and it is also home to the chough, a rare, red-billed crow. A square tower near the harbour was the stronghold of Grace O'Malley, the 16th-century pirate who declared herself queen of Clew Bay and held her own against Elizabeth I on a visit to London in 1575.

THE SOUTHWEST

A cable-car links **Dursey Island** to the mainland off the tip of the Beara Peninsula in Co Cork. Popular with birdwatchers, who climb the western cliffs to observe gannets and search for rare migrants, the island has no paved roads. Transport between the three tiny villages is by motorcycle or horse-drawn vehicle.

Cape Clear, Ireland's southernmost island, challenges the Atlantic from Roaringwater Bay in West Cork. About 5km long, the island is wild and precipitous, but there are tiny pastures

and its houses are protected by hedges of fuchsia and escallonia. During the summer its population of 150 is swollen by the visitors, naturalists and Irish language students who travel by ferries from Schull and Baltimore.

Celtic crosses at dawn on Inishmore, the largest of the Aran Islands

ARAN ISLANDS
There are regular air services from Galway some 50km away. Ferry services operate from Doolin, Co Clare (tel: 065–74455), Galway City (tel: 091–68903) and Rossaveal, Co Galway (tel: 091–61767). Heritage Centre, Inishmore – tel: 091–63081 for opening hours. There is no traffic on Inishmaan and Inisheer.

CLARE ISLAND
Clare has a twice-daily ferry service from Roonah Quay (tel: 098–25711). The trip takes 25 minutes.

DURSEY ISLAND
Cable car – tel: 064–41233.

CAPE CLEAR
Ferries: Schull – tel: 028–28138
Baltimore – tel: 028–39119.

WATERWAYS

You don't have to drive very far in Ireland before encountering a lough (lake) or river. But why drive? Both the Republic and Northern Ireland offer alternatives in the form of waterway holidays. Vital in the days before the railways, the waterways have become a rich legacy of leisure, affording a relaxing opportunity to gain a backyard view of Ireland at its best.

The Republic has three major waterway systems, each connected to the other. From Dublin, the Grand Canal runs westwards to meet the stately River Shannon. Less than halfway along its route, a branch of the canal goes off to meet the River Barrow, which provides a navigable route south to Waterford.

Northern Ireland has Lough Erne – Upper and Lower – a superb lakeland cruising area, with an island, they'll tell you, for every day of the year.

Thanks to restoration work on a derelict canal, the Shannon-Erne

GRAND CANAL
A boat hire just outside the town offers English-style narrowboats. Celtic Canal Cruisers, Tullamore, Co Offaly (tel: 0506–21861).

RIVER SHANNON
Nine companies offer nearly 400 self-skippered boats for hire on the Shannon. Information from Bord Fáilte offices (see page 189).

RIVER BARROW
Celtic Canal Cruisers – see **Grand Canal** above.

LOUGH ERNE
Lakelands Visitor Centre, Shore Road, Enniskillen, Co Fermanagh (tel: 01365–323110/325050).

Clonmacnois monastic settlement on the banks of the mighty River Shannon

Waterway now connects the River Shannon with Lough Erne, enabling boaters to cruise freely over some 800km between the provinces of Leinster, Munster and Ulster.

THE GRAND CANAL

Between Lucan, just outside Dublin, and Shannon Harbour there are only 24 locks in a distance of about 125km. Robertstown, where the River Barrow link starts, is an attractive village with a boating centre and a base for hiring cruisers. Edenderry, on a spur off the canal's main line, has excellent moorings in a pleasing harbour. Tullamore is the home of *Tullamore Dew* whiskey and the liqueur, *Irish Mist*. Shannon Harbour, marking the entrance to Ireland's major river, was once a thriving inland port. Now it provides a safe haven for many boaters.

What a catch! Fishing at Lough Erne

RIVER SHANNON

The Shannon contains the largest area of inland waters in Britain and Ireland. It flows southwards for 350km, following the course of history between Co Cavan, where it rises, and the Atlantic Ocean. It passes through only one city – Limerick – but it provides an opportunity to view and visit some of Ireland's finest historical sites, including the stunning Clonmacnois (see pages 50–1), the most important early Christian monastic settlement. Carrick-on-Shannon, a popular starting point for cruising holidays, has some fine Georgian buildings.

Along its length, the Shannon has a wealth of birdlife and flora, and it is flanked by ancient woodlands. There are nature trails to explore at Portumna Castle, on the shore of Lough Derg, and in Lough Key Forest Park.

RIVER BARROW

The river passes through many fascinating places. Athy is a market town whose history goes back to medieval times. Carlow has a Norman castle. Graiguenamanagh is a photogenic town with the restored Duiske Abbey, founded in 1207. St Mullins, near the end of the navigation, has associations with early Celtic mythology.

LOUGH ERNE

Cruising offers the best way to see many of Fermanagh's attractions. Mooring up at Devenish and White Islands, for example, enables you to view their mysterious ruins and relics without the crowds. Devenish is wonderful by moonlight (see page 109). Navigation throughout the Erne system is easy and boating facilities are excellent.

HIKING AND CYCLING

Great country for walking and cycling, in mountain, forest, glen and valley, can be found throughout Ireland. The Ulster Way, an 800km footpath, follows the Northern Ireland coastline, returning to Belfast through the Sperrin Mountains, the Fermanagh Lakeland and the Mountains of Mourne.

Year-round walking and rambling tours are organised by the Youth Hostel Association of Northern Ireland. Specialists who arrange walking holidays of various grades, with or without a guide, are listed in the Irish Tourist Board's brochure, *Walking Ireland – Only the Best.*

A dozen marked trails range from the Burren Way (23km) to the Kerry Way (215km). Some organised walks have a base, with daily walks. Post-to-post walking is available in some areas with luggage transported from base to base.

Hikers' accommodation can usually be found near trails. Most farmers allow overnight camping if asked. Self-guided trails or guided walks are available in Ireland's national parks.

Most of Ireland's roads, being

relatively free of motor traffic, are a joy for cyclists, and many areas are ideal for all-terrain bikes, which can be hired in the north and south. An Enniskillen hire company also organises day trips, two- and seven-day sightseeing tours and family fun runs.

INFORMATION
Ulster Way Sports Council for Northern Ireland, House of Sport, Upper Malone Road, Belfast BT9 5LA (tel: 01232–381222).
National Park Office of Public Works, 51 St Stephen's Green, Dublin 2 (tel: 01–661 3111).
Raleigh Rent-a-Bike Kylemore Road, Dublin 10 (tel: 01–626 1333); The Bike Store, 58 Lower Gardiner Street, Dublin 1 (tel: 01–872 5931).
Cycling Safari Holidays 31 Chanterhill Park, Enniskillen, Co Fermanagh, BT74 4BG (tel: 01365–323597).

Ireland is a marvellous country for walking, hiking and rambling

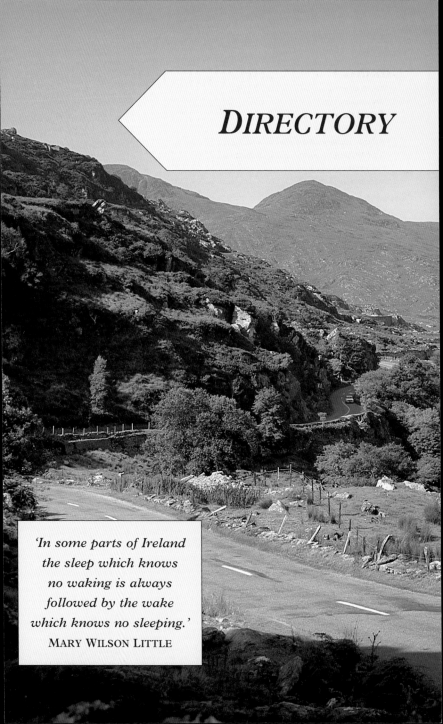

DIRECTORY

'In some parts of Ireland
the sleep which knows
no waking is always
followed by the wake
which knows no sleeping.'
MARY WILSON LITTLE

Shopping

*M*any of the souvenirs on sale to visitors are bought at shops within craft centres, factories and mills, after they have seen the goods at various stages of production. Some of these shops stock a range of products made elsewhere in Ireland. Good quality mementoes and gifts are also on sale at Tourist Offices.

Both Belfast and Dublin have compact city centres. Both cities have some splendid multi-floor, covered shopping centres – among them Westbury Mall and the Powerscourt Centre in Dublin, and Castle Court in Belfast.

Belfast's waterfront redevelopment scheme includes some up-market shops within a conference centre, concert hall and hotel complex.

Belfast is the traditional home of Irish linen, and this can be found in several of the city's arcades and pedestrianised area shops. Handmade woollens, pottery and glassware – Tyrone Crystal is made in Ulster (see page 111) – are welcome gifts. Smithfield Arcade in Belfast is popular for seeking out bargains, and market addicts should not miss the

A shop sign as good as the contents of the window

Friday morning St George's variety market at May Street.

In Dublin, pedestrianised Grafton Street and its environs, and wide O'Connell Street, are the main places for the committed shopper, with windows displaying classic clothes and exciting new styles, and designer knitwear. Nearby Nassau Street has a parade of shops, some of which are still in the hands of the families that founded them. Exquisite woollens and tweeds are on sale. One shop sells men's and women's suits, jackets and hats in handwoven Donegal tweed, and lengths of tweed can be bought, so that customers can have them made up when they get home.

Cork City shops are mostly small and interesting, each retailer an expert in his or her field. High quality fashions are elegantly displayed cheek by jowl with bookshops, tobacconists, pharmacies, hardware stores, toy shops and jewellers. Crescent-shaped St Patrick's Street is the main shopping thoroughfare, and a pedestrianised area is flanked by Carey's Lane, French Church Street and Paul Street.

Several craft studios have been set up in the Bridge Mills in Galway, by O'Brien's Bridge. The converted 18th-century mill also houses a wine bar and second-hand bookshop.

Waterford City presents itself as the 'Shopping Capital of the Southeast', and is indeed a vibrant centre with a range of specialist outlets lining its narrow streets.

There are bargains for dedicated shoppers, from books to traditional Irish knitwear

Waterford Crystal heads the field (see page 66), but there are several other centres in which quality crystal is created. Pottery, already firmly established in some areas – Belleek is the best-known (see pages 108–9) – is a developing craft. Studios producing functional and decorative pottery are opening all over the country.

You can still see handmade Irish harps, made in Mayo, Meath and Dublin. Craftsmen in Limerick, Clare and Cork make chairs and stools in local ash or beech. Burnished blackthorn is used for walking sticks. Good examples of the blacksmith's craft – fire irons and ornamental ironwork – are produced in Cork and Kerry.

Jewellery in silver, gold and enamel is created in unusual and classic designs. The famous Claddagh ring – the lovers' symbol of two hands cradling a crowned heart – can be found in sterling silver.

Basket weaving and rushwork are homecrafts producing a variety of goods, including tablemats. Among other crafts practised around the country are batik work – fairly new to Ireland – stained glass, tapestry, fly-tying and leather-work.

Sligo's three-week Shopping Spree in the autumn, has bargains all over town. It culminates in a Shoppers' Auction.

Throughout the country many of the shops selling crafts and goods of Irish manufacture run a mailing service.

Visitors from overseas may reclaim the cost of Value Added Tax (VAT) on purchases made in the Republic and Northern Ireland.

SHOPS

Countless shops throughout Ireland offer crafted gifts and souvenirs. There is not the space here to mention more than a few outlets selling Ireland's high quality products. For information on local outlets for a particular purchase inquire at the nearest tourist office.

ANTIQUES

BELFAST
Belfast Antiques Market
Stamps, coins, furniture, toys.
126 Donegall Pass, Belfast 7. Tel: 01232–232041. Saturdays only.

CO ANTRIM
Country Antiques
Silver, porcelain, furniture.
219b Lisnevenagh Road, Antrim. Tel: 01849–462498

CO CORK
Victoria's
Period clothes, Victoriana.
2 Oliver Plunkett Street, Cork. Tel: 021–272752.

CO DONEGAL
The Gallery
Paintings, antiques, crafts.
Dunfanaghy. Tel: 074–36224.

CO DUBLIN
Mother Redcap's Indoor Market
Antiques, crafts, paintings and other wares.
Back Lane, Christchurch, Dublin 8. No telephone.

CO FERMANAGH
Ballindullagh Barn
Curios, crafts and paintings in an off-the-beaten-track 18th-century barn.
Killadeas. Tel: 01365–621548.

ART

CO KERRY
Blennerville Studio
Oils, watercolours, stonecraft, original art based on local landscapes, prints and pottery.
1 Main Street, Blennerville. Tel: 066–31824.

Killarney Art Gallery (Mulvany Bros)
The work of Irish painters is on sale here.
47 High Street, Killarney. No telephone.

BOOKS

CO DUBLIN
Eason's
Four spacious floors of books, stationery, posters, souvenirs and other goods.
O'Connell Street, Dublin 1. Tel: 01–873–3811.

Fred Hanna
Books of Irish interest. Huge range on most subjects.
27–9 Nassau Street, Dublin 2. Tel: 01–677 1255.

Hodges Figgis
One and a half million books stocked – if it's not here, the management claims, then it simply does not exist.
54 Dawson Street, Dublin 2. Tel: 01–677 4754.

Winding Stair
Interesting Liffey-side second-hand book store.
40 Lower Ormond Quay, Dublin 1. Tel: 01–873 3292.

CRAFTS

BELFAST
Craftworks Gallery
Government-sponsored with wide range of Northern Ireland crafts on sale.
13 Linenhall Street, Belfast 2. Tel: 01232–236534.

CO CLARE
Gleninagh Crafts
Stained-glass products and unusual items – mobiles, lamps, candle holders.
Fiontrach, Ballyvaughan. Tel: 065–77154.

CO CORK
Blarney Woollen Mills
Much more than woollens – a wide selection of Ireland's goods.
Blarney. Tel: 021–385280. Also 21–3 Nassau Street, Dublin 2. Tel: 01–671 0068.

Trag Knitwear
Hand- and machine-knit Aran sweaters. Fashions, crafts. Bargain basement.
Tragumna, Skibbereen. Tel: 028–21750.

CO DONEGAL
Magee
Department store. Established 1866. Magee's hand-woven tweed is still made in cottages and finished in the factory. High-grade men's and women's clothing.
The Diamond, Donegal. Tel: 073–21100.

McAuliffe's Craft Shop
Hand-woven rugs. Men's and women's clothes in Irish textiles. Crystal.
Dunfanaghy. Tel: 074–36135.

Teresa's Cottage Industries
Embroidered table linen, luncheon sets and cushion covers. Place mats, bed linens, knitwear.
Church Street View, Bruckless. Tel: 073–37080.

Triona Design
Weaving demonstrations. Factory shop. Ladies' fashions in tweed; other Irish products.
Ardara. Tel: 075–41422.

CO DUBLIN
Gaelic Design Sweater & Gift Shop
Souvenirs from Guinness boxer shorts to *bodhrans* (small, single-skin drums). Also classy cottons, tweeds and knitwear.
Asdills Row, Temple Bar, Dublin 2. Tel: 01–671 1146.

CO KERRY
Quill's Woollen Market
Claims the best selection of designer handknits and woollen goods – and keenest prices. Also in Sneem and Kenmare.
Killarney. Tel: 064–32277.

CO SLIGO
Innisfree Crystal
Many limited editions which can only be purchased at the factory.
The Bridge, Collooney. Tel: 071–667340.

CO WATERFORD
Joann's Gift Shop
Waterford and Galway mouth-blown, hand-cut crystal. Belleek, Royal Tara and Donegal chinas.
29–30 Michael Street, Waterford. Tel: 051–73138.

JEWELLERY
CO DONEGAL
McElwee
Crystal from Waterford, Tipperary and Derryveagh. China and ironstone ware. Rynhart bronze sculptures.
Dungloe. Tel: 075–21032.

CO SLIGO
Gillan Jewellery Designs
Hand-crafted silver and gold. Work by other Irish artists.
Market Yard, Sligo. Tel: 071–43686.

W F Henry
Large range of jewellery and watches, including Claddagh rings in gold and silver.
1 High Street, Sligo. Tel: 071–42658.

TEXTILE CRAFTS

Crafts usually develop where the raw materials are available. It follows, therefore, that homespun tweeds and woollens were traditionally based in noted sheep-rearing areas like Donegal, Galway, Kerry, Mayo and Wicklow. Each region had its distinctive product, depending not only on the local wool used, but also on the local dyes.

In parts of Donegal, long famous for its strong tweed, hand-weaving continues as a

cottage industry. The crafts of hand knitting and hand embroidery are still found here. In the same areas, workshops can be visited where a new generation of weavers produces lighter, brighter textiles – scarves, dress lengths, rugs and wall hangings.

Aran jerseys are never out of fashion, though they owe their origin to the fact that they are practical – thick, warm and rain-resistant – and

Ireland has a reputation for excellent quality textiles, many produced using the time-honoured traditional ways

process in linen manufacturing. Wellbrook Beetling Mill, near Cookstown, Co Tyrone, opens for limited hours on summer afternoons and is well worth a visit (see page 112).

The Middle House Museum, at Upperlands, Maghera, Co Londonderry, has a private textile museum opened by appointment by the Clark family, who live there. The machinery dates from 1740 (tel: 0648–42214 to arrange a guided tour).

Yarn was bleached by boiling, and laid out to dry on 'bleach greens'. Northern Ireland had about 360 bleach greens in the industry's late 18th-century heyday.

ideal for wintry sea fishing trips in an open boat. Even the intricate patterns devised by families and passed down from one generation to the next were rooted in practicality, if a somewhat morbid one. It is said they were a means of identifying drowned fishermen.

Irish hand crochet work is a much sought-after fashion accessory today.

Weaving in linen is now limited to Northern Ireland. A little flax is still grown there, but most is imported. Beetling – hammering the cloth to produce a smooth sheen – is the final

Entertainment

*I*reland does not immediately spring to mind when planning a holiday with a sizzling nightlife, but you would be wrong to dismiss it altogether.

Much of the nightlife is impromptu. A lot of it takes place in pubs and bars; places where people know they can relax over a drink in pleasant company, chat with acquaintances or strangers, and where there is always a chance of someone striking up a tune on a tin whistle, a guitar or fiddle, or even the uilleann pipes. And suddenly there's a sing-song, a 'session' they call it.

This is the 'crack', the good-time fun factor, and if you don't want strong drink you can get it with tea or coffee. To go to Ireland and not visit the bars is as unthinkable as going to Egypt without seeing the pyramids.

But if you want organised entertainment, the best you can expect outside Dublin, Belfast and the main centres is the cinema, bingo, bowling, possibly an evening of amateur folk dancing in a local hall, or a disco where anyone over 30 may be considered geriatric.

The answer for those wanting to dance until dawn, to take in a night at the opera or theatre, or to hear a top-class rock band or international orchestra is to come to Ireland in July or August. They do get big-name, high calibre entertainment here, but it may not coincide with a visit outside the peak holiday season.

To find out what is on, keep an eye on the local newspapers which carry advertising and editorial information on entertainments taking place in the area. For more detailed news of what to see and do call at the tourist information office. Apart from leaflets on local attractions and festivals, free newspaper-style publications, such as the *Cork and Kerry Tourist News* and the *Northern Ireland Holiday News*, are a mine of information.

Entire regions, like the Northwest (Sligo, Donegal and district) and Shannon (Clare, Limerick, North Kerry, North Tipperary and South Offaly) are covered in annual visitors' guides. Many small towns have a privately published free sheet, like the *Tralee Advertiser.*

In Northern Ireland, the 20-page *Lakeland Extra* is distributed to homes and businesses in Fermanagh and South Tyrone, and can also be picked up at various locations, including

Dublin's National Concert Hall – a magnificent setting for musical performances

The Manhattan night club, Belfast, where you can dance the night away

tourist information centres.

There is every chance you will find something of interest in these publications, but don't expect it to keep you riveted until the small hours. You could be in bed by 10pm.

The advice given in one of the free monthly papers for visitors is: 'Rest well to prepare for another day of fun and adventure in the region that nature has indeed given more than its fair share.' And why should anyone argue with that?

Apart from the minute terrorist fraternity on both sides of the community, the Irish are a people who love everybody.

They really do make you feel supremely welcome. Nobody who seeks company is allowed to be lonely in Ireland.

It is not that they are curious about you. They are not nosy. They do not intrude. They just recognise you are someone to talk to, and the talk is never trite or tedious. It is straight from the heart, it is anecdotal, informative, showing interest in your responses, your impressions of Ireland and the Irish. It leads to humour, wit and laughter, it extends to others in your proximity – be it at bus stop or bar – and suddenly you are enjoying yourself enormously.

WHAT'S ON

Many of the entertainments listed here take place only during the summer, and others, like live music in pubs, are limited to fewer appearances. It is wise to check beforehand.

AMUSEMENT CENTRES

See page 150.

BANQUETS

CO CLARE

Bunratty Castle
Twice-nightly medieval banquet year round.
Bunratty. Tel: 061–61788 for reservations.
Bunratty Folk Park Ceilidh Evenings
Irish stew and Irish singing and dancing.
Bunratty. Tel: 061–61788 for reservations.
Knappogue Castle
Twice-nightly banquets with musical entertainment May to October.
Quin. Tel: 061–61788 for reservations.

CO GALWAY

Dunguaire Castle Medieval Banquet
Extracts from works of Synge, Yeats and Gogarty. Twice nightly (times: 5.45 and 8.45pm) May to September.
Kinvara. Tel: 061–61788 for reservations.

CO KERRY

Killarney Manor
Five-course banquet with Irish music, song and dance in 18th-century Great Hall.
Loreto Road, Killarney. Tel: 064–31551.

BOWLING

CO FERMANAGH

Castle Bowlervision
Ten lanes of ten-pin bowling.
Castle Entertainment Centre, Raceview, Factory Road, Enniskillen. Tel: 01365–324172. Open: daily 9am–2am.

CO LIMERICK

Limerick Leisure Bowl
Twenty computerised lanes. Gym, sauna and dance classes.
Ennis Road, Limerick. Tel: 061–327444.

CO WATERFORD

Clonea Strand Hotel
Bowling alley.
Dungarvan. Tel: 058–42416.

CABARET

BELFAST

Limelight
Disco/nightclub. Cabaret Tuesday, Friday and Saturday.
Ormeau Avenue. No telephone.

CO DUBLIN

Abbey Tavern
Fun, laughter and traditional singing.
Howth. Tel: 01–839 0307.
Braemor Rooms
Home-reared stars and some from the world stage.
Churchtown, Dublin 14. Tel: 01–298 8664.
Jury's Irish Cabaret
Sparkling 2½-hour entertainment, May to mid-October.
Jury's Hotel, Pembroke Road, Ballsbridge, Dublin 4. Tel: 01–660 5000.
Pink Elephant
Young set's venue with up-and-coming rock singers and those who have arrived.
South Frederick Street, Dublin 2. Tel: 01–677 5876.

CO LIMERICK

Jury's Hotel
Music, song, dance, comedy and drama at Jury's Summer Show: Thursday nights in June and September, Wednesday and Thursday in July and August.
Ennis Road, Limerick. Tel: 061–327777.

CONCERTS AND OPERA

BELFAST

Grand Opera House
See pages 98 and 145.

Queens University School of Music
Admission charge for evening concerts.
Free lunchtime recitals autumn/winter.
*University Square/Botanic Avenue. Tel:
01232–245133, ext 3480, for information.*

Ulster Orchestra
*Ulster Hall, Bedford Street. Tel: 01232–
664535 for ticket information.*

CO CORK

Cork Opera House
Irish plays predominate in summer.
Opera, ballet, musical comedy.
Lavitt's Quay, Cork. Tel: 021–270022.

CO DUBLIN

National Concert Hall
Leading venue for classical music.
*Earlsfort Terrace, Dublin 2. Tel: 01–
671 1888.*

CO LONDONDERRY

Guildhall
Concerts and dramatic productions.
*Shipquay Street, Londonderry. Tel:
01504–365151.*

HOTEL ENTERTAINMENT

CO CLARE

Bunratty Castle Hotel
Garfield's Cabaret and Niteclub open to
the small hours Friday and Saturday.
Bunratty. Tel: 061–364116.

Lakeside Hotel
Cast of talented singers, musicians, step-
dancers and comedians in cabaret. Late
June to early September.
Killaloe. Tel: 061–376122.

West Country Hotel
Ballads, step-dancing, drama and
comedy in cabaret: Tuesdays in June,

Tuesday and Friday from July to
September.
Ennis. Tel: 065–28421.

CO DUBLIN

Harcourt Hotel
Chiki's Nightclub, open Thursday to
Sunday. Country/bluegrass with Sunday
brunch; jazz Sunday and Monday nights.
*60–1 Harcourt Street, Dublin 2. Tel: 01–
478 3677.*

CO GALWAY

Peacocke's
Irish Night Saturdays, disco Friday and
Sunday 10pm–2am.
Maam Cross. Tel: 091–82306.

CO KERRY

Ballybunion Golf Hotel
Baby-sitting service. Nightly
entertainment.
*Main Street, Ballybunion. Tel: 068–
27111.*

Eviston House Hotel
Danny Mann Singing Lounge,
Scoundrels Niteclub.
New Street, Killarney. Tel: 064–31640.

Hotel Gleneagle and Leisureworld
Wings Nightclub with top names.
Nightly music and sing-along in summer
at Eagles Whistle pub.
*Muckross Road, Killarney. Tel: 064–
31870.*

Killarney Towers Hotel
Scruffy's Music Bar nightly.
*College Square, Killarney. Tel: 064–
31038.*

CO LIMERICK

George Hotel
Tropics Nightclub, open nightly, and
Glory Hole Music Pub.
*O'Connell Street, Limerick. Tel: 061–
414566.*

THE PUBS

People rave about Ireland's pubs and bars – the 'crack' (conversation and good-time factor), the character, the generally easy-going ambience. And justifiably. That is not to say, however, that some of them don't have dismal décor, plastic upholstery and archaic fittings.

The trouble is, most have frosted windows or are heavily curtained, so you can't tell what they're like until you go in. However, at least three times out of four you'll be successful, and even the dreary ones usually have friendly staff and customers.

The traditional snug areas are still a feature of many old pubs – closed-in

sections where a few friends can get together in relative privacy. There are plenty about. William Blake's, Church Street, in Enniskillen is one. In Dublin's Baggot Street Lower there's Doheny and Nesbitt's. Another is Kehoe's, in South Anne Street, Dublin, whose snugs were immortalised by Sean O'Casey.

The Crown Liquor Saloon in Great Victoria Street, Belfast, is the city's most flamboyant. It was built in 1885 by an architect who was inspired by what he had seen in Spain and Italy. The result is red and yellow ceilings, marble-topped bar with wooden arches and columns, and panelled snugs with ornate carvings over the doors. The pub is cared for by the National Trust, whose restoration work includes gas lamps (see page 98).

Some Irish pubs have a theme. Carmichael's of Holywood, Co Down, near the Belfast-Bangor railway, serves food and drink in what resembles railway carriages.

Music is a big attraction in many pubs – dozens of them in Dublin. Slattery's, in Capel Street, has traditional Irish music, rock and blues entertainment seven nights a week. Concerts are given at Bad Bob's Backstage Bar in Essex Street East, where traditional and folk, country and jazz are also played.

Many world-famous singers and bands started as pub musicians in Ireland.

Pubs are an institution in Ireland and an essential element of daily life. A visit is a pleasant way of getting to know the people

NIGHTCLUBS
BELFAST
Larry's Piano Bar
Lively atmosphere, '30s Bohemian-style extravagance, piano music.
34 Bedford Street. Tel: 01232–325061.

Live music at Larry's Piano Bar

Pips Nightclub
Located in a complex which includes Elbow's pub, a popular venue for music.
Dublin Road. Tel: 01232–233003.

CO DONEGAL
Frankie's Niteclub
Tuesday teenagers' disco (no alcohol), disco nights Wednesday, Friday and Saturday, and Irish Country and Western bands on Saturday.
Meeting House Street, Raphoe. Tel: 074–45153.

CO FERMANAGH
Mirage
Features talented performers and the country's first seven-colour graphic laser system.
Castle Entertainment Centre, Raceview, Factory Road, Enniskillen. Tel: 01365–324172.

CO LIMERICK
Baker Place
Pub/restaurant with late-night dancing.
Perry Square, Limerick. Tel: 061–418414.

CO LONDONDERRY
Squires Nightclub
Young people's rendezvous.
Shipquay Street, Londonderry. Tel: 01504–266017.

PUB ENTERTAINMENT
BELFAST
Kelly's Cellars
Saturday afternoon folk, Saturday night blues.
30 Bank Street, Belfast 1. Tel: 01232–324835.
The Linenhall
Live jazz on Monday, Wednesday and Saturday; rock on Thursday.
Clarence Street, Belfast 1. Tel: 01232–48458.
Rotterdam Bar
Irish, folk, blues or jazz most nights.
54 Pilot Street, Belfast 1. Tel: 01232–746021.

CO CLARE
Archway
Restaurant/bar with great music.
Main Street, Ennistymon. Tel: 065–71080.

CO DONEGAL
Shamrock Lodge
Traditional Irish music, Wednesday and Saturday all year.
Falcarragh. Tel: 074–35192.

CO DUBLIN
International Bar
Lively venue for rock bands and other groups. Wednesday comedy night.
23 Wicklow Street, Dublin 2. Tel: 01–677 9250.

The Crown Liquor Saloon, a fine example of an ornate, gaslit Victorian pub

Slattery's

Paul Brady performed here regularly 30 years ago. Still a top choice for rock, blues, trad and folk.
Capel Street, Dublin. Tel: 01–872 7971.

CO LIMERICK

Nancy Blake's
Traditional music Sunday to Wednesday in one of the city's foremost bars.
Denmark Street, Limerick. Tel: 061–416443.

CO LONDONDERRY

Dungloe Bar
One of the town's best pubs for music and quizzes.
Waterloo Street, Londonderry. Tel: 01504–267716.

Townsman
Popular nightspot with young people.
33 Shipquay Street, Londonderry. Tel: 01504–260820.

CO SLIGO

Knock na Shee Inn
Ballads, traditional Irish music, sing-songs.
Lavagh, Ballymote. Tel 071–84001.

Yeats Lounge
Ceilidh every Friday night. Music at weekends.
Rathcormac. Drumcliff. Tel: 071–43039.

THEATRES

BELFAST

Grand Opera House
Plays, opera, ballet and pantomime.
Great Victoria Street, Belfast 1. Tel: 01232–241919.

Lyric Theatre
Drama based on Irish heritage.
Ridgeway Street, Belfast 7. Tel: 01232–381081.

CO CORK

Cork Opera House
Variety, touring productions.
Lavitt's Quay, Cork. Tel: 021–270022.

CO DUBLIN

Abbey Theatre
Drama based on Irish culture.
Lower Abbey Street, Dublin 1. Tel: 01–878 7222.

Gate Theatre
Contemporary plays.
Cavendish Row, Parnell Square, Dublin 1. Tel: 01–874 4045.

Olympia Theatre
Comedy, dance, drama – you name it.
Dame Street, Dublin 2. Tel: 01–677 7744.

CO KERRY

Siamsa Tíre National Folk Theatre
Summer music, folklore, song, dance.
Tralee. Tel: 066–23055.

MUSIC, MUSIC, MUSIC!

You know it when you hear it – you can't stop your feet tapping. Traditional Irish music is difficult to define, but easy to enjoy.

Although each new Irish generation promotes its own interpretation of traditional music, and adds to the range of ballads, there has been a swell in the trend in recent years.

Notes of political strife, emigration and rebellion against authority creep into ballads. Overtones of bawdiness and lust have never been away, and the sad solos of unrequited love, lost love and thwarted love continue to sell in mega-figures.

Irish singers and performers and Irish groups have worldwide impact. Music reverberates in the pubs and in the streets. Sometimes it is impromptu. Often it is 'all join in'.

The harp – the instrument most readily associated with Ireland – is seldom played as a traditional instrument today, though a musician playing one in Dublin's Grafton Street attracts huge crowds. The fiddle is at the hub of traditional Irish music.

The *uilleann* pipes, with the elbow used to pump air, are a refined version of bagpipes, and the *bodhran* – a small goatskin drum – is popular in West Cork and Kerry. It is beaten with the

In a pub, or out in the street, any time is a good time for music

Traditional music has a high profile
in Ireland

Irish harp maker, tuning a new instrument
at Marlay Park, Dublin

knuckles or a soft, double-ended
drumstick.

The tin whistle provides a merry
accompaniment to other instruments,
and the accordion and flute are often
played solo.

The Republic has a central
organisation for promoting music, song
and dance – the Comhaltas. Its annual
booklet, a guide to traditional music
organised by Comhaltas branches
nationwide, is available free from
tourist information centres.

At the end of August the three-day
All-Ireland Fleadh (pronounced *flah*),
held in a different location each year,
marks the highlight of the traditional
music calendar.

Festivals and Events

*F*estivals large and small are staged throughout Ireland to celebrate activities, interests and anniversaries ranging from the cultural to the practical, from the commonplace to the bizarre. Whatever the event – whether it is concerned with horses or roses, art or oysters – it will almost certainly involve music, often traditional, and it will definitely be fun.

Here is a month-by-month round-up of some of the major events staged annually in both the Republic and Northern Ireland. Some are held in a different location each year, and dates may drift into the previous or succeeding month. Tourist offices will have up-to-date information.

January
The Royal Dublin Society's Irish Crafts Fair, Dublin; major horse races at Gowran Park (Co Kilkenny), Leopardstown (Co Dublin), Naas (Co Kildare) and Thurles (Co Tipperary).

February
International Arts Festival, Dublin; Dublin Film Festival, Dublin; Punchestown bloodstock sales, Naas, Co Kildare; Ulster Harp National steeplechase, Downpatrick, Co Down; Ulster Motor Show, Belfast.

March
Belfast Musical Festival; Heavy Horse Show and ploughing match, Ballycastle, Co Antrim; St Patrick's Day (17 March) celebrations held throughout Ireland – big parades in Belfast and Dublin; pilgrimages at Cultra, Downpatrick and Newry, all in Co Down.

April
Arklow Music Festival, Co Wicklow; Belfast Civic Festival and Lord Mayor's Show; Dublin International Piano Competition; Irish Grand National, Fairyhouse, Co Meath; Pan Celtic Week, Republic; World Irish Dancing Championships, Republic.

May
Bantry Mussel Festival, Co Cork; Cork International Choral Festival; Dundalk International Maytime Festival, Co Louth; Fermanagh Lakelands Fishing Festival; Fleadh Ceoil (festival of traditional music, song and dance), Republic; Royal Ulster Agricultural Society Show, Belfast; Spring Show and Industries Fair, Dublin.

June
Budweiser Irish Derby, The Curragh, Co Kildare; Bloomsday (16 June), celebration of James Joyce's *Ulysses,* Dublin; Dun Laoghaire Festival, Co Dublin; Feis na nGleann (traditional music, dancing, sport), Glens of Antrim; Festival of Music in Great Irish Houses, Republic; Fiddle Stone Festival – gathering of Irish fiddlers at Belleek, Co Fermanagh; Listowel Writers Week; Lough Swilly International Tope Festival, Rathmullen, Co Donegal.

July
Bray Seaside Festival, Co Wicklow; Cork International Folk Dance Festival; Galway Arts Festival; Galway Races; King of Dalkey Festival, Co Dublin; City of Belfast International Rose Trials; Medieval Fair, Carrickfergus, Co Antrim;

Battle of the Boyne Commemoration (Orangemen's Day – 12 July), Northern Ireland; Skibbereen Welcome Week, Co Cork.

August

Ancient Order of Hibernians' Parades (15 August, Feast of the Assumption), Northern Ireland; Connemara Pony Show, Clifden, Co Galway; Dublin Horse Show; Kilkenny Arts Week; Mary from Dunloe International Festival,

Autumn Season, Grand Opera House, Belfast; Waterford International Festival of Light Opera.

October

Ballinasloe International October Fair – one of Europe's biggest traditional horse and cattle fairs, Co Galway; Cork International Film and Jazz Festivals; Dublin City Marathon; Kinsale Gourmet Festival, Co Cork; Sligo Arts Festival.

Dixon Park is host to the City of Belfast's International Rose Trials every July

Dunlow, Co Donegal; O'Carolan Harp and Traditional Music Festival, Boyle, Co Roscommon; Oul' Lammas Fair, Ballycastle, Co Antrim; Puck Fair, Killorglin, Co Kerry; Relief of Derry Celebrations commemorating siege of 1688–9; Rose of Tralee International Festival, Co Kerry; Skibbereen Horse Fair, Co Cork.

September

Belfast Folk Festival; Clarinbridge Oyster Festival, Co Galway; Dublin Flower Show; Matchmaking Festival – the ultimate singles party, Lisdoonvarna, Co Clare; Opera Northern Ireland

November

Belfast Festival – a cornucopia of music, from classical to jazz, as well as drama, opera and cinema in and around Queen's University; Wexford International Opera Festival.

December

Christmas horseracing, Leopardstown, Co Dublin; New Year Viennese Ball, Belfast City Hall; Wren Boys Festival, Bunratty Folk Park, Co Clare. Wren Boys in fancy dress and with blackened faces traditionally sing and dance in the streets and demand money (for charity nowadays).

Children

AMUSEMENT CENTRES

Children of any age will enjoy a visit to one of the amusement parks, where attractions range from slides and pools to rides and arcades.

Leisureland Amusement Park
Wide selection of rides, waterslides and heated indoor pool.
Salthill, Galway.

Mack's Amusements
Videos, slot machines, children's rides, bingo. Open 10am–midnight.
Main Street, Bundoran, Co Donegal.

Tramore Amusement Park
Many rides and attractions. Tramore seafront also has a miniature railway.
Seafront, Tramore, Co Waterford.

Tropicana
Slides, adventure playground, variety shows, drama, films.
Central Promenade, Newcastle, Co Down.

Waterworld
An indoor complex with an 80m water flume, whirlpools, entertainment with water cannon and pirate ship and relaxing saunas and jacuzzis to provide a contrast. Also under cover is a funfair.
Portrush, Co Antrim.

BEACHES

Given good weather – and that is something that cannot be taken for granted in Ireland – many children are happy to spend time paddling in the sea and building sandcastles on the lovely and often uncrowded beaches. But the time comes when they want a little more adventure and excitement.

The vast majority of Irish beaches – they call them strands – remain delightfully natural. But in the shadow of the Binevenagh Mountain at Lough Foyle, Co Londonderry, lie 5km of clean sand, the Strand of Benone, and adjacent to it is the **Benone Tourist Complex**. Here smaller children can splash about under supervision in heated pools, while older ones can enjoy the thrills of the adventure playground.

Portrush has generous lengths of sandy beach, with donkey rides and candy floss.

The busy seaside resort of Bundoran, Co Donegal, has its own Waterworld, an indoor heated **Aqua Adventure Playground** on the seafront. It has a wave pool and a slide for small children,

The traditional seaside resort of Newcastle

as well as a choice of long, short, fast, slow, straight or spiral slides.

Tramore, Co Waterford, has a wide sweep of beach, a miniature railway and an amusement park.

BOAT TRIPS/WATERSPORTS

Most children love a boat trip. In Glengarriff, Co Cork, boatmen vie for the privilege of transporting summer visitors – at a negotiable fee – to **Garinish Island** in Bantry Bay, a 10- to 15-minute ride away. Seals are often seen swimming, or basking on rocks. Italian gardens, including subtropical plants, are the big attraction on the island. Children can explore woodland paths, a Grecian-style temple and a Martello tower (see page 70).

Another interesting boat cruise goes past the wooded islands of **Killarney's Lower Lake**.

You can hire rowing boats or canoes in many towns and villages situated on rivers, canals or lakes.

Sea canoeing is an option at a few centres. At **Marble Hill Strand**, 6km east of Dunfanaghy, Co Donegal, children over 10 can receive instruction and go on a supervised expedition. Windsurfing is also taught. Wetsuits and equipment can be hired.

CAVES

Caves are always fascinating. Among the most dramatic are **Marble Arch Caves,** near Blacklion, Co Fermanagh – part of the tour is by electric boat (see page 110) – and **Aillwee Cave,** Ballyvaughan, Co Clare, inhabited long ago by brown bears (see page 75).

HORSE RIDING

Ireland has residential riding centres where instruction is given, or where trail riding is offered. There are also non-residential centres which take novices, including children, for basic instruction by the hour.

MUSEUMS

Many of the exhibits at Belfast's **Ulster Folk and Transport Museum** appeal to children, and on Saturdays in summer a miniature railway operates (see page 103).

Belfast Zoo

ZOOS AND WILDLIFE

Belfast Zoo is on Cave Hill – the higher you go the steeper it gets (see page 96). **Dublin Zoo,** in Phoenix Park, opened more than 160 years ago (see page 27). Along Northern Ireland's Causeway Coast, off the B62 Ballymoney-Portrush road, is the **Causeway Safari Park.** Lions roam free as you drive through the wooded reserve. A mini zoo and children's amusements are on site (see page 115). **Westport House,** Westport, Co Mayo, has a zoo and a wonderfully equipped children's playground (see page 84). Visitors can watch the milking routine from a gallery, see animals and poultry and follow a nature trail at **Streamvale,** Northern Ireland's first open dairy farm, at Ballyhanwood Road, Dundonald, Belfast (closed: November to January.)

Sport

SPECTATOR SPORTS

Ireland generally manages to maintain a reasonably high profile in international sports – especially rugby and soccer – but traditional games continue to attract a huge following. The most striking characteristics of traditional games are the fervour and sportsmanship of the players and the exemplary behaviour of the fans. The all-Ireland finals of the Gaelic Games inter-county championships are played in September, usually at Croke Park, Dublin.

BULLETS

The strangest sport – and from the spectator's point of view, potentially most dangerous – is bullets, or road bowls, which entails throwing a metal ball weighing almost 1kg over a course covering several kilometres of winding public roads. People say the game was originally played with cannonballs. Once played throughout Ireland, bullets is mostly confined to the lanes of Counties Armagh and Cork, but it is also played in many small towns and villages. Some tournaments attract teams from Gaelic communities abroad.

GAELIC FOOTBALL

Gaelic football, a hybrid of soccer and rugby, is played with a round ball and involves two 15-strong teams whose members may handle the ball.

HORSERACING

Ireland has 28 courses, offering racing over 230 days of the year. Sunday racing has been introduced in recent years, and evening meetings are held from May to August. The headquarters of Irish racing is the Curragh, Co Kildare, where the Budweiser Irish Derby is run in June. Another classic, the Guinness Oaks, is held at the Curragh in July.

The two-day Irish Grand National event takes place at Fairyhouse, Co Meath, at Easter. Other national hunt courses are at Galway, Gowran, Navan and Punchestown.

Festival meetings are held during the summer and early autumn at Galway, Killarney, Listowel, Tralee and Tramore. The Irish Point-to-Point season of rural steeple chases runs from January to May. Events are staged every Sunday.

A calendar giving full details of racing is available from the Racing Promotion Group, Leopardstown Racecourse, Foxrock, Dublin 18 (tel: 01–289 7277).

In Northern Ireland the major event is the Ulster Harp National steeple chase, staged at Downpatrick.

The Irish National Stud and the Irish Horse Museum are both at Tully, Co Kildare (tel: 045–21617). The museum tells the story of the Irish horse from prehistoric times. Its centrepiece is the skeleton of the famous racehorse, Arkle.

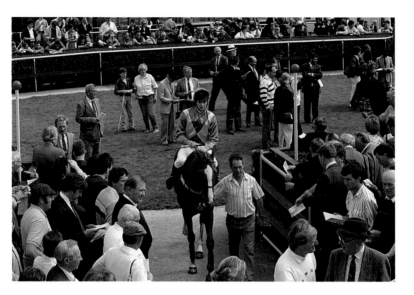

HURLING

The national game is hurling. An ancient game – it is mentioned in early Irish legends – hurling looks like a cross between rugby, hockey, lacrosse and guerrilla warfare. Played between teams of 15 burly men (there is a women's version, called camogie), it is said to be the world's fastest field game. The players belt a small leather ball with hockey-like sticks. The ball may be caught but not thrown. Hurling fields, found all over the Republic and in some parts of Northern Ireland, look like rugby pitches except that goalposts are netted below the crossbar.

RUGBY

Local matches are played at weekends throughout the Republic and Northern Ireland. In Dublin, international matches take place at the Lansdowne Road stadium. Details of fixtures can be found in the national and local press.

Racing is hugely popular in Ireland and a major social event

SHOWJUMPING

Showjumping is one of Ireland's main weekend attractions, with more than 500 events taking place each year, some held in conjunction with agricultural shows. Country shows offer an attractive spectacle and provide an insight into Irish rural life. A full list of shows is available from the Showjumping Association of Ireland, Anglesea Lodge, Anglesea Road, Dublin 4 (tel: 01–660 1700).

SKITTLES

Another traditional game now being revived in Ulster is crossroads skittles. Popular before the advent of television in Cavan, Donegal, Fermanagh, Leitrim and Monaghan, the game is re-emerging at fairs and festivals, and championships have been staged in Co Fermanagh.

PARTICIPATORY SPORTS

Fresh air and fitness are easy to find in
Ireland, where the opportunities for
outdoor pursuits are immense. Indoor
facilities – swimming pools and gymnasia
– are found in many luxury and resort
hotels.

EQUESTRIAN SPORTS

Ireland and the horse are synonymous,
and there are riding centres, residential
and non-residential, everywhere. Even
those visitors staying in Dublin or Belfast
will not have far to travel to get into the
saddle.

Among some 20 or so establishments
in the Dublin area are the Carrickmines
Equestrian Centre, Glenamuck Road,
Foxrock, Dublin 18 (tel: 01–295 5990)

and Brooke Lodge Riding Centre,
Stepaside Stables, Burrow Road,
Stepaside (tel: 01–295 2153).

Belfast's closest riding establishment
is the year-round Lagan Valley
Equestrian Centre, 172 Upper Malone
Road, Belfast 17 (tel: 01232–614853).
Closed Sunday.

Trail-riding with overnight
accommodation in farmhouses, country
homes and hotels, or at stay-put centres,
is available in many rural areas.

Arrangements can also be made for

visitors to participate in hunting.

Information on riding holidays can
be obtained from any Irish Tourist
Board or Northern Ireland Tourist
Board office, or from the Association of
Irish Riding Establishments, 11 Moore
Park, Newbridge, Co Kildare (tel:
045–31584).

Ireland's sporting facilities are second
to none

GOLF

There are around 250 golf courses in
the Republic and a further 80 or so in
Northern Ireland that welcome visitors.
Those in the Dublin area include the
Royal Dublin Golf Club, North Bull
Island (tel: 01–833 6346) and the
Arnold Palmer-designed course at the
Kildare Hotel and Country Club,
Straffan, Co Kildare (tel: 01–627 3111).
Belfast has about a dozen clubs within
8km of the city centre. Information is
available from main tourist offices

SAILING

Ireland's varied coastline – to say
nothing of its many lakes – offers
everything from windsurfing and
dinghy-sailing to sedate cruising and
rugged ocean racing.

The most popular cruising area,

between Cork Harbour and the Dingle Peninsula, offers 143 totally different places where a boat can moor safely and peacefully for an overnight stay. Harbours like Youghal, Dunmore East and Kinsale extend a welcome to yachtsmen in their friendly bars and restaurants.

Sailing schools are located at a number of places on the Irish Sea and Atlantic coasts. Information can be obtained from the Irish Association for Sail Training, Confederation House, Kildare Street, Dublin 2 (tel: 01–677 9801).

The Irish Tourist Board issues a leaflet with details of yacht charter companies. In Northern Ireland the Lakelands Visitor Centre, Shore Road, Enniskillen, Co Fermanagh, (tel: 01365–323110) will have information on watersports facilities on Lough Erne.

TENNIS

Although the Irish climate is often unsympathetic, tennis is gradually growing in popularity. Public courts can be found in the cities and larger towns, and about 100 hotels have grass or hard courts.

Dublin is well served, with public facilities at Bushy Park (tel: 01–490 0320), Herbert Park (tel: 01–668 4364) and St Anne's Park (tel: 01–831 3697).

For futher information contact Tennis Ireland, Argyle Square, Donnybrook, Dublin 4 (tel: 01–668 1841).

FISHING

Few countries offer such a profusion of well-stocked fishing waters as Ireland, and few market their angling facilities so expertly or so affordably. Festivals and competitions in coarse, game and sea angling are open for visitors. Sea angling and coarse fishing are year-round activities in Ireland.

For fishing in private water, the permission of the owner must be obtained. A licence is not required for sea fishing.

In the Republic be sure to stay at accommodation registered with and approved by Bord Fáilte. Specialist accommodation offers such amenities as meals served to suit ideal local fishing times, copious hot water, a rod room and overnight clothes drying. Your gamefish catch can be deep frozen or smoked to take home.

For the *Angler's Guide to Ireland,* listing approved accommodation, write to Bord Fáilte (Irish Tourist Board), Baggot Street Bridge, Dublin 2 (tel: 01–602 4000). Also available are free *Ireland Angling – Only the Best* information sheets, with maps, on coarse, game and sea angling.

The Northern Ireland Tourist Board publishes *Where to Stay in Northern Ireland,* listing a range of accommodation. The book may be ordered with a cheque or postal order for £3.99 sterling or equivalent from the Tourist Information Office, NITB, St Anne's Court, 59 North Street, Belfast BT1 1NB (tel: 01232–231221/246609). The NITB also issues free Information Bulletins on sea fishing from boats (No 9), fishing from the seashore (No 10), game fishing (No 23) and coarse fishing (No 28).

For the addresses of overseas offices of both boards see page 189.

For the latest information on licensing and permits contact either the appropriate Tourism Information office of the Fisheries Conservancy Board (rod licences) or the Department of Agriculture (permits).

ADDRESSES
Fisheries Conservancy Board
1 Mahon Road, Portadown,
BT62 3EE
(tel: 01762–334666);
Department of Agriculture
(Fisheries), Stormont, Belfast
BT4 3PW
(tel: 01232–763939).

ADVENTURE PURSUITS

Mountains in Ireland are mostly well-rounded ranges rather than high jagged peaks, which means an absence of vicious air currents.

Add the facts that most of the hills are free of trees, power lines and other encumbrances and that many of them provide a soft landing on peat, and it is clear that Ireland has near-ideal conditions for gliding and hang-gliding. On good days pilots can enjoy soaring for hours at a time. There are guided tours between March and September and tuition is available.

Parachuting, which for the dedicated enthusiast can lead to skydiving, takes place at weekends in Ireland's two centres. A first-timer can jump from an aircraft after a day's training.

Few hills and mountains of Ireland exceed 920m but they provide interesting climbs, beauty and solitude. Mountain rescue teams with helicopter back-up operate in the main areas.

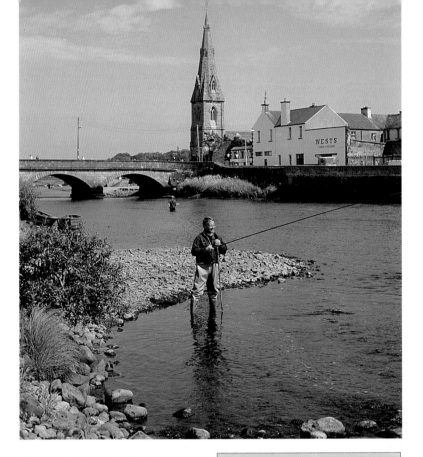

Ballina stands at the mouth of the Moy, one of the country's best salmon rivers

Because there are few tracks, maps and compasses should always be carried.

Canoeing is one of Ireland's fastest-growing sports, on coastal and inland waters. It takes place all year. As well as touring and camping by canoe – the option of most visitors – there are summer marathons, flat-water sprints and, for the highly skilled, surfing.

White-water racing – timed runs over very rough stretches of river – and slaloms are other exciting aspects of canoeing.

ADDRESSES
Irish Hang-Gliding Association
Irish Canoe Union, Parachute Association of Ireland, and Hill Walking and Rock Climbing are all at: House of Sport, Long Mile Road, Walkinstown, Dublin 12.
Tel: 01–450 1633 (hang-gliding and canoeing). Tel: 01–450 9845 (parachuting and rock climbing).
Ulster Gliding Club
(Alan McKillen), 80 Rathmore Road, Bangor, Co. Down.
Tel: 01247–457794.

Food and Drink

*P*laces to eat out in the Republic and Northern Ireland vary from coffee shops and pubs to high-class restaurants and the occasional castle offering medieval-style dining. Generally, prices are lower in the North. It is wise to book in advance or arrive early for anything but the most casual of evening meals – this applies particularly on Sundays in the North where some places are closed. Some restaurants, including those in hotels in both North and South, serve food nearly all day – luncheons, snacks and high tea – then close their dining room at 7 or 8pm. Except in the fashionable parts of major cities, people tend to eat early.

Expect to pay around £2 for a pint of Guinness – other stouts may be cheaper. Some unlicensed premises don't mind you bringing your own wine.

The £ symbol is used as an approximate guide to the price bracket of each place listed – for a three-course meal per person, excluding wine or coffee. In the Republic the symbol represents the punt. Service charges, if they exist, vary, so check the menu.

£ = under £10
££ = £10–£15
£££ = £15–£20
££££ = over £20

LEINSTER
DUBLIN CENTRAL
Ante Room Seafood Restaurant ££
Also vegetarian, Irish beef and lamb.
20 Lower Baggot Street, Dublin 2. Tel: 01–661 8832.

Bad Ass Cafe £
The pizzeria for fun and noise – video, juke box, music. Demijohns of wine.
9–11 Crown Alley, Dublin 2. Tel: 01–671 2596.

Brokers Restaurant ££
Fully licensed Irish family restaurant. Traditional food and vegetarian.
25 Dame Street, Dublin 2. Tel: 01–679 3534.

Le Caprice £££
Italian/Continental. Pastas, veal, vegetarian.
12 St Andrew's Street, Dublin 2. Tel: 01–679 4050.

The Cedar Tree Lebanese Restaurant ££
Authentic Lebanese cuisine and vegetarian dishes in Arabian-style 'cavern'.
11a St Andrew's Street, Dublin 2. Tel: 01–677 2121.

Chapter One £££
Irish and Continental cuisine, vegetarian. Based on Dublin Writers' Museum.
18–19 Parnell Square North, Dublin 2. Tel: 01–873 2266.

The Commons Restaurant ££££
Classic international food.
Newman House, 85–6 St Stephen's Green, Dublin 2. Tel: 01–475 2597. Closed: Sunday.

Dillon's Restaurant ££
Irish stew, steaks, fish, vegetarian.
21 Suffolk Street, Dublin 2. Tel: 01–677 4804.

Old Dublin Restaurant ££££
Russian and Scandinavian cuisine, fish a speciality.
91 Francis Street, Dublin 8. Tel: 01–454 2028/454 2346. Closed: Sunday.

Polo's ££££
Go for the décor and modern artwork as well as the Californian/Continental fare.
Schoolhouse Lane, off Molesworth Street, Dublin 2. Tel: 01–676 6442/676 3362. Closed: Sunday.

Restaurant Tosca £
Pasta, pizza, casual Italian eating all day till late.
20 Suffolk Street, Dublin 2. Tel: 01–679 6744.

The Shelbourne Hotel Dining Room ££££
Modern Irish cuisine in historic hotel.
27 St Stephen's Green, Dublin 2. Tel: 01–676 6471.

DUBLIN SOUTH

Chandni's Restaurant ££
Noted Tandoori food accompanied by sitar music.
174 Pembroke Road, Ballsbridge, Dublin 4. Tel: 01–668 9088. Closed: Sunday lunchtime.

Ernie's ££££
Designed around a mulberry tree. Many Irish paintings displayed. Charcoal grills, game in season.
Mulberry Gardens, Donnybrook, Dublin 4. Tel: 01–269 3300/269 3260. Closed: Sunday and Monday.

Jury's Hotel and Towers (Coffee Dock) ££
Top-grade hotel with three restaurants, as well as this coffee shop. Snacks and full meals.
Ballsbridge, Dublin 4. Tel: 01–660 5000. Open: 6am–4.30am the next day, from Tuesday to Saturday; 7am–11pm Sunday and Monday.

Kitty O'Shea's ££
Spacious 200-seat restaurant of the Parnell era – late 19th-century.
23–5 Upper Grand Canal Street, Dublin 4. Tel: 01–660 9965/660 8050.

Locks £££
Small French provincial-style restaurant by Grand Canal. Classical and modern cuisine.
1 Windsor Terrace, Portobello, Dublin 8. Tel: 01–454 3391/453 8352. Closed: Saturday lunchtime and Sunday.

Sachs £££
Small, Georgian-style restaurant serving fish, steaks, poultry, vegetarian and gluten-free dishes.
Donnybrook, Dublin 4. Tel: 01–668 0995.

Good solid fare – Irish stew is traditionally made with lamb

Ireland is renowned for its excellent salmon and variety of seafood

DUBLIN NORTH
Brahms & Liszt ££
Family restaurant near Dublin Airport.
Extensive choice of food, competitively
priced.
*Swords Road, Santry, Dublin 9. Tel:
01–842 8383.*

CO CARLOW
The Lord Bagnel Inn ££
Good food in pleasant atmosphere.
Leighlinbridge. Tel: 0503–21668.

CO DUBLIN
Abbey Tavern ££££
Turf fires, original stone walls, flagged
floors and gaslights. Fish a speciality.
*Abbey Street, Howth. Tel: 01–839 0307.
Closed: Sunday.*
Ayumi-Ya Japanese Restaurant £££
Japanese cuisine. Teppan-Yaki, sushi,
vegetarian.
*Newpark Centre, Newtown Avenue,
Blackrock. Tel: 01–283 1767.*
Bon Appetit ££££
Fresh seafood, veal, steaks, duck. Also
vegetarian and gluten-free dishes.
*9 James Terrace, Malahide. Tel: 01–
845 0314/845 2206. Closed: Sunday.*

Cooper's Wine Bar ££
Indian, Chinese and European food in
converted 18th-century premises.
*8 The Crescent, Monkstown. Tel: 01–
284 2037/284 2995.*
De Selby's ££
Reasonable prices and personality.
Vegetarian and gluten-free dishes.
*17–18 Patrick Street, Dun Laoghaire.
Tel: 01–284 1761/2.*
Healy's Black Lion Inn ££
Founded in 1838, the inn specialises in
steaks and seafood.
*Orchard Road, Main Street, Clondalkin,
Dublin 22. Tel: 01–457 4814/457 4253.
Open: noon–11.30pm (10.30pm on Sunday).*
Howth Lodge Hotel Restaurant £££
AA 3-star family-run hotel serving
charcoal-grilled fresh fish and steaks.
Howth. Tel: 01–832 1010.
Red Bank Restaurant ££££
Chef/proprietor cooks catch of the day,
landed at the pier each evening.
*7 Church Street, Skerries. Tel: 01–849
1005. Closed: Sunday and Monday.*
Roches Bistro £££
French cooking in view of customers.
*12 New Street, Malahide. Tel: 01–
845 2777.*

Stillorgan Park Hotel
(The Carvery Room) ££
Great value. Noted for prime rib beef.
Stillorgan. Tel: 01–288 1621. Closed:
Saturday lunchtime.
Truffles Restaurant ££££
Fresh local game and seafood.
Fitzpatrick's Castle Hotel, Killiney. Tel:
01–284 0700.

CO KILDARE
Red House Inn £££
Haute cuisine; home-grown vegetables.
Turf fires.
Newbridge. Tel: 045–31516/31657.
Closed: Sunday and Monday.
Springfield Hotel £££
Family-run hotel. Vegetarian dishes.
Leixlip. Tel: 01–624 49265. Open: 12.30
–11.30pm.

CO KILKENNY
Mount Juliet Hotel (Lady Helen
McCalmont Restaurant) ££££
Fine linen, crystal and silverware reflects
quality cuisine.
Thomastown. Tel: 056–24455.
Parliament House £££
Victorian ambience. Vegetarian and
gluten-free dishes available.
24–5 Parliament Street, Kilkenny. Tel:
056–63666.

CO WESTMEATH
The Castle Pantry ££
Quality home-cooking in a 600-year-old
castle. Vegetarian dishes.
Tyrrellspass Castle. Tel: 044–23105.
Jolly Mariner ££
Large, pleasant restaurant beside the
River Shannon. Vegetarian dishes
available.
Abbey Road, Athlone. Tel: 0902–
721113/728892. Closed: Monday and
Tuesday (except June to August).

CO WEXFORD
The Bohemian Girl ££
The owner/chef prepares meat and
seafood and has been a frequent award
winner.
North Main Street, Wexford. Tel: 053–
24419.
Hotel Rosslare £££
Award-winning bar food. Restaurant
handy for ferryboat passengers.
Opposite Rosslare Harbour. Tel: 053–
33110.

CO WICKLOW
Pizza del Forno ££
Restaurant/steakhouse/pizzeria.
The Mall Centre, Main Street, Wicklow.
Tel: 0404–67075.
Tree of Idleness ££££
International gourmet dishes, including
Greek. Award-winning wine list.
Seafront, Bray. Tel: 01–286 3498/
282 8183. Closed: Monday.

MUNSTER
CO CLARE
Auburn Lodge Hotel ££
Irish and international food; vegetarian
dishes.
Galway Road, Ennis. Tel: 065–31247.
Bali Room Restaurant £££
Indonesian and Irish fare in small
friendly restaurant.
Weaver Inn, Newmarket-on-Fergus.
Tel: 061–368114. Closed: Sunday.
Crotty's £
This combined pub/guesthouse is noted
for excellent simple fare and legendary
traditional music sessions.
Kilrush. Tel: 065–52470
Dromoland Castle ££££
Impressive chandeliers and candles
provide the romantic setting for a special
night out.
Newmarket-on-Fergus. Tel: 061–71144.

CO CORK

Barn Restaurant £££
Fresh Irish produce, distinctive cuisine.
Lotamore, Glanmire. Tel: 021–866211.

Bistro Seafood Winebar £££
Specialising in fresh local produce.
Guardwell, Kinsale. Tel: 021–774193.
Closed: Monday to Saturday lunchtime.

Blarney Park Hotel
(Clancarthy Restaurant) ££
Wholesome food in relaxed surroundings.
Blarney. Tel: 021–385281.

Casey's Cabin ££
Go for the view and the seafood.
Baltimore. Tel: 028–20197. Closes: 9pm.
Also closed Sunday 2–5pm.

Castle Hotel ££
Family-run hotel which has won awards
for its tourist menu.
Macroom. Tel: 026–41074. Closes: 8.30pm.

Dun-Mhuire Restaurant ££
Fish a speciality. Vegetarian available.
Kilbarry Road, Dunmanway. Tel: 023–
45162. Closed: Sunday to Tuesday.

Doloree House £££
Continental finesse to fresh local
produce. Vegetarian, gluten-free dishes.
Lisavaird, Clonakilty. Tel: 023–34123.
Closed: Monday (except Bank Holidays).

Finins £££
Quality food, bar menu.
75 Main Street, Midleton. Tel: 021–
631878/632382. Closed: Sunday.

John Barleycorn Inn £££
Steaks, fresh fish. Vegetarian and gluten-
free dishes.
Riverstown, Glanmire. Tel: 021–821499.

McCarthy's ££
Good, old-world atmosphere.
Blackrock Castle, Blackrock, Cork City.
Tel: 021–357414/358109. Closed:
Monday, and Tuesday for dinner.

Tung Sing ££
Chinese restaurant on Cork's main
thoroughfare.
23a Patrick Street, Cork. Tel: 021–
274616.

Vickery's Inn £££
Varied menus while bar food is served
all day.
New Street, Bantry. Tel: 027–50006.

Victoria Hotel ££
Vegetarian meals on menu.
Macroom. Tel: 026–41082.

Westlodge Hotel £££
Seafood a speciality. Children are well
catered for.
Bantry. Tel: 027–50360.

GOURMET CAPITAL

Kinsale is the haunt of epicures from
around the world early in October
when this fishing port holds an
international four-day Gourmet
Festival. Throughout the year the
ancient town attracts discerning
diners, having firmly established itself
as Ireland's Gourmet Capital.

In 1975, 12 restaurants got together
to form the Kinsale Good Food Circle,
and excellent seafood is served at all
of them. Vegetarians can always find
something tasty and unusual, like the
nettle soup and courgette and herb
bake at the Cottage Loft, Main Street.
Locally picked wild spinach and locally
farmed mussels are featured on the
menu at the Blue Haven, on the site of
the old fishmarket. Walnut soup is an
interesting starter at The Captain's
Table in Acton's Hotel, and a
memorable monkfish in tarragon
sauce and white wine is served at
Max's Wine Bar, in Main Street.

Windmill Tavern £££
Seafood and gourmet cooking.
46 North Street, Skibbereen. Tel: 028–21606. Closed: Sunday in winter.

CO KERRY

Arbutus Hotel (Pat's Restaurant) £
Fresh, home-made meals.
College Street, Killarney. Tel: 064–31037.

Beginish Restaurant £££
Emphasis on seafood.
Green Street, Dingle. Tel 066–51588. Closed: Monday.

Chez Jean-Marc £££
Imaginative French cuisine.
29 Castle Street, Tralee. Tel: 066–21377. Closed: Sunday.

**Eviston House Hotel
(Colleen Bawn Restaurant) £££**
Fine food in elegant surroundings.
New Street, Killarney. Tel: 064–31640. College Street, Killarney. Tel: 064–33404.

Kiely's Restaurant ££
Very extensive dinner and à la carte.
College Street, Killarney. Tel: 064–31656.

Mickey Neds £
Home-made dishes and delicatessen fare in a friendly atmosphere.
Henry Street, Kenmare. Tel: 064–41591.

The Three Mermaids £££
Award-winning pub/restaurant.
William Street, Listowel. Tel: 068–21184/22443.

CO LIMERICK

The Castle Oaks Hotel £££
Georgian-style dining room.
Castleconnell. Tel: 061–377666.

Mustard Seed £££
Over 100 dishes offered in village house with original Irish kitchen.
Adare. Tel: 061–396451. Closed: Sunday, Monday, and all of February.

Patrick Punches ££
Roasts, prime steaks, seafood.

Punches Cross, Limerick. Tel: 061–27149/29588.

Shangrila ££
Peking and Cantonese dishes.
103 O'Connell Street, Limerick. Tel: 061–414177.

CO TIPPERARY

**Buttermarket Restaurant
'La Scala' ££**
Friendly, family-run restaurant.
Vegetarian dishes.
Market Street, Clonmel. Tel: 052–24147. Closed: Sunday evening.

The Fox's Den £££
Cellar-like restaurant with character.
Modreeny, Cloughjordan. Tel: 0505–42210 (after 2.30pm). Closed: Sunday, and Monday evenings.

Gurthalougha House ££££
Candle-lit dinner served nightly at 8pm in country house dining room. Booking essential. Quay for cruisers.
Ballinderry, Nenagh. Tel: 067–22080.

CO WATERFORD

Dwyers of Mary Street ££
Quiet little restaurant with short but impact-making menu.
8 Mary Street, Waterford. Tel: 051–27478/21183. Closed: Sunday.

Merry's ££
Seafood restaurant in 17th-century wine merchant's store. Bar food all day.
Lower Main Street, Dungarvan. Tel: 058–41974/42818.

The Ship £££
Extensive menu includes seafood, vegetarian.
Dunmore East, Waterford. Tel: 051–83141/83144.

Waterford Castle £££
Chef Paul McCloskey uses local organic produce.
The Island, Ballinakill. Tel: 051–78203.

CONNACHT
CO GALWAY
Boluisce Cottage Bar ££
Award-winning seafood bar and restaurant. Vegetarian dishes.
Spiddall Village, Connemara. Tel: 091–83286.

Connemara Coast Hotel (The Gallery) £££
Views over Galway Bay, original paintings displayed. Live piano music.
Furbo. Tel: 091–92108.

Dun Aonghusa ££
Restaurant overlooking Galway Bay.
Kilronan, Inishmore, Aran Islands. Tel: 099–61104.

Galleon Restaurant £
Reputation for good Irish stew, fish and steaks at budget prices.
Salthill, Galway. Tel: 091–521266/522963. Open: to midnight.

Glynsk House £££
Lobster, salmon, oysters, mussels, shrimps and other seafood.
Carna Road, Cashel, Connemara. Tel: 095–32279.

Lydon's ££
Family restaurant. Children welcome.
5 Shop Street, Galway. Tel: 091–564051/566586.

Meadow Court Restaurant/Bar £££
Multi award-winning establishment specialising in fresh seafood and extensive international cuisine.
Loughrea. Tel: 091–841051/841633.

Owenmore Restaurant ££
Country house restaurant serving fresh home-made dishes; local seafood a speciality.
Ballynahinch Castle, Recess, Connemara. Tel: 095–31006. Closed: February.

Paddy Burkes £££
Connoisseurs from around the world experience the Clarenbridge oyster here. Steaks and seafood.

The Oyster Inn, Clarenbridge. Tel: 091–796226.

Peacocks ££
Fresh fish and quality steaks competitively priced.
Maam Cross. Tel: 091–82306.

CO MAYO
The Moorings ££
Cordon bleu cooking, fresh local ingredients in family restaurant.
The Quay, Westport. Tel: 098–25874. Closed: Sunday.

Swiss Barn Speciality Restaurant £££
Small, highly rated restaurant offering fondues, lobster thermidor, home-made ice creams.
Foxford Road, Ballina. Tel: 096–21117. Closed: Monday (except Bank Holidays).

CO SLIGO
Dragon House Restaurant ££
Cantonese, seafood, vegetarian dishes.
17 Temple Street, Sligo. Tel: 071–44688/44696.

ULSTER
BELFAST CENTRAL
Fat Harry's £
Steaks, grills.
91 Castle Street, Belfast 1. Tel: 01232–232226. Open: in the evening to 9pm.

Front Page £
Prawns in garlic and haddock mornay are among specials. Vegetarian dishes.
106 Donegall Street, Belfast 1. Tel: 01232–324269. Open: Monday to Saturday noon–9.30pm.

Nick's Warehouse ££
Try warm salad of pigeon breast with balsamic dressing, or smoked salmon mousse with smoked salmon as a starter. Imaginative vegetarian food.
35–9 Hill Street, Belfast 1. Tel: 01232–439690. Closed: Saturday and Sunday.

BELFAST – GOLDEN MILE
Arthur's ££
Try seafood mousse profiteroles or pork escalope with Stilton and raspberry sauce.
7 Hope Street, Belfast 2. Tel: 01232–333311. Closed: Sunday.
Bananas ££
Good continental and oriental food.
4 Clarence Street, Belfast 2. Tel: 01232–339999. Closed: Sunday.
La Belle Epoque £££
French cuisine, game in season.
61 Dublin Road, Belfast 2. Tel: 01232–331532.
Café Orleans £
Pasta, steaks and seafood.
34 Bedford Street, Belfast 2. Tel: 01232–325061. Closed: Sunday and Monday.
Charmers ££
Try the stuffed mushrooms or pavlova.
85 Dublin Road, Belfast 2. Tel: 01232–238787. Closed: Sunday.
China Town £
Good Cantonese.
60 Great Victoria Street, Belfast 2. Tel: 01232–230115.
House of Moghul ££
Indian and European food.
60 Great Victoria Street, Belfast 2. Tel: 01232–243727.
Roscoff ££££
Proprietor Paul Rankin trained under master chef Albert Roux.
7 Lesley House, Shaftesbury Square, Belfast 2. Tel: 01232–331532. Closed: Sunday.

BELFAST – UNIVERSITY AREA
The Ashoka ££
Indian and European cuisine. Presents a food festival Sunday and Monday in summer.
363 Lisburn Road, Belfast 9. Tel: 01232–660362.

Chez Delbart ££
French bistro – crêpes, baked mussels.
10 Bradbury Place, Belfast 7. Tel: 01232–38020.
Dukes Hotel ££££
Modern French-style cooking using quality Ulster ingredients. Extensive wine list.
65 University Street, Belfast 7. Tel: 01232–236666.
Errigle Inn ££
Live music, roof garden.
320 Ormeau Road, Belfast 7. Tel: 01232–641410.
Maloney's ££
Opened in 1991. Crab en croûte, crème bavarois.
33 Malone Road, Belfast 9. Tel: 01232–682929. Closed: Sunday lunchtime.
New Jade Palace ££
Chinese, Cantonese and European.
717 Lisburn Road, Belfast 9. Tel: 01232–381116.
Saints & Scholars ££
Deep-fried Irish brie a speciality.
3 University Street, Belfast 7. Tel: 01232–325137.

Fresh oysters and Guinness are served in many pubs and hotels round Galway

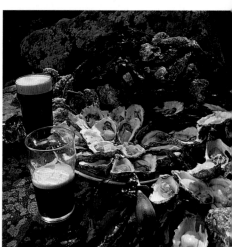

BELFAST – EAST OF THE RIVER LAGAN

Four Winds Inn £££
Open fires provide cosy atmosphere. Evening à la carte.
111 Newton Park, Belfast 8. Tel: 01232–401957 Closed: Sunday.

BELFAST NORTH

Ben Madigan ££££
On the slopes of Cave Hill with views over city and coast. Taste of Ulster member.
Belfast Castle, Antrim Road, Belfast 15. Tel: 01232–776925.

Strathmore Inn £
Steaks, grills. Salads, set lunch, à la carte.
192 Cavehill Road, Belfast 15. Tel: 01232–391071.

CO ANTRIM

Adair Arms Hotel ££
Lobster soup, snails in garlic butter, à la carte.
Ballymoney Road, Ballymena. Tel: 01266–653674. Last orders: 9.30pm weekdays, 7.45pm Sunday.

Angelo's Ristorante £
Cannelloni, lasagne. Unlicensed, but clients welcome to bring own wine.
3 Market Lane, Lisburn. Tel 01846–672554. Closed: Sunday and Monday.

Ballyarnott House £££
Home cooking.
Oldstone Hill, Antrim. Tel: 01266–63292. Closes: 9pm.

Bushmills Inn £££
Gas lighting, peat fires, local products used. Speciality – River Bush salmon and Bushmills whiskey.
25 Main Street, Bushmills. Tel: 01265–732339.

Carriages £
Tasty grills and pizzas.
105 Main Street, Larne. Tel: 01574–275132. Closed: Sunday lunchtime.

Chimney Corner Hotel ££
Steaks, grills. Quick service, handy for international airport. Good à la carte menu.
630 Antrim Road, Glengormley. Tel: 01232–844925.

Dionysus ££
Greek and English. Good mezze and souvlaki.
53 Eglinton Street, Portrush. Tel: 01265–823855.

Ginger Tree £££
Japanese.
29 Ballyrobert Road, Ballyclare. Tel: 01232–848176. Closed: Sunday.

Grouse Inn ££
Wood-panelled Bailiff's Parlour Restaurant, also grill bar. Fresh local seasonal ingredients.
2–12 Springwell Street, Ballymena. Tel: 01266–45234. Closed: Sunday.

Harbour Inn £
Fresh seafood.
5 Harbour Road, Portrush. Tel: 01265–825047.

Hillcrest Country House ££
Close to Giant's Causeway, panoramic coastal views. Noted for seafood and sauces.
306 Whitepark Road, Bushmills. Tel: 01265–731577. Open: weekends only November to April.

Jim Baker Restaurant £
Quick grills in bowling stadium.
Ballysavage Road, Parkgate, Templepatrick. Tel: 01849–432927. Closed: Sunday.

Londonderry Arms ££
Fresh, simple fare, home-style cooking in former coaching inn. Excellent home-made bread.
20–8 Harbour Road, Carnlough. Tel: 01574–885255.

Lotus House ££
Chinese and European.
58 Bow Street, Lisburn. Tel: 01846–678669.

Magherabuoy House Hotel £££
View over the coast. Fresh baked salmon.
Magheraboy Road, Portrush. Tel: 01265–823507.

Sleepy Hollow £££
Try pigeon breasts in red wine. Also includes an art gallery within the restaurant.
15 Kiln Road, Newtownabbey. Tel: 01232–342042. Open: Wednesday to Saturday 7–9.30pm.

Templeton Hotel £££
All tastes catered for, including vegetarian. Local specialities. À la carte.
882 Antrim Road, Templepatrick. Tel: 01849–432984.

The Wallace £££
Small restaurant with imaginative menu, frequently changed.
12–13 Bachelor's Walk, Lisburn. Tel: 01846–665000. Closed: Sunday evening.

Welcome ££
Chinese and European.
16 Bridge Street, Portadown. Tel: 0762–332325.

Waterford and Limerick are well known for their fine cooked hams

CO ARMAGH

Carngrove Hotel ££
Menu includes duckling, paella, à la carte.
2 Charlestown Road, Portadown. Tel: 01762–339222.

Digby's & Red Grouse £
Steaks, kebabs.
53 Main Street, Killylea. Tel: 0861–568330. Closed: Monday and Tuesday evenings.

Drumhill House Hotel ££
Salmon, lobster.
35 Moy Road, Armagh. Tel: 01861–522009. Last orders: 9.30pm.

Rainbow £
Chinese and European.
59 Scotch Street, Armagh. Tel: 01861–26556.

CO DONEGAL

Danby Restaurant £££
Extensive menu using own garden vegetables and herbs.
Rossnowlagh Road, Ballyshannon. Tel: 072–51138. Closed: Sunday.

Danny Minnies £££
Pancakes a speciality. Peat fire in cosy inglenook.
Teach Killendarragh, Annagry. Tel: 075–48201.

Errigal Restaurant £
Family, with good selection of food, keenly priced. Children's menu.
Main Street, Donegal. Tel: 073–21428.

Strand Hotel £££
Variety of home-cooked dishes served in this family-owned hotel.
Ballyliffen. Tel: 077–76107.

WATER OF LIFE

Old soldiers know that you should never volunteer for anything. Old soldiers can be wrong. Lucky (or opportunist) volunteers visiting the Irish Whiskey Corner in Dublin (see page 30), or the Jameson Heritage Centre at Midleton, Co Cork (see page 70), face a rare tasting challenge – to choose their favourite from among five popular Irish whiskeys and compare them with a Scotch or Bourbon. Many people have been known to change the drinking habit of a lifetime.

Spelling apart, Irish is distinctively different from Scotch whisky. In Scotland, the malted barley which forms the basis of the spirit is dried over an open peat fire, imparting its characteristic smoky flavour. The Irish dry theirs in smoke-free kilns,

producing a clear, clean barley taste. Another difference is that Irish whiskey is distilled three times, while most similar spirits produced elsewhere are distilled only twice.

The art of distillation was discovered long ago in the Middle East – Aristotle mentioned the process in the 4th century BC – but it was first used for making perfume.

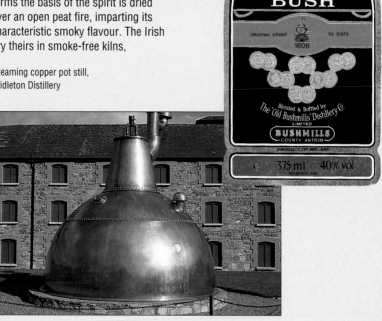

Gleaming copper pot still,
Midleton Distillery

The Irish soon found a better use for it when distillation was introduced by Christian missionaries around AD600. They found a good name for the new product, too – 'Water of Life'. English soldiers serving in Ireland in the 12th century shortened the Irish phrase *Uisce Beatha* (pronounced Ish'ke Ba-ha)

to whiskey, and the word stuck.

Ireland once had more than 2,000 distilleries. Today, there are only two – at Midleton and Bushmills, Co Antrim. Bushmills, licensed since 1608, is Ireland's oldest legal distillery (see page 115). Like Midleton and the Irish Whiskey Corner, it has a visitor centre.

CO DOWN

Abbey Lodge Hotel ££
Fresh oysters, crêpes.
Belfast Road, Downpatrick. Tel: 01396–614511. Last orders: 9.30pm.

Adelboden Lodge £££
Simple home cooking, including vegetarian menu. Chef/proprietor Margaret Waterworth is known for her wholemeal wheaten bread.
38 Donaghadee Road, Groomsport. Tel: 01247–464288. Closed: Sunday and Monday.

Burrendale Hotel £££
Good food and warm welcome.
51 Castlewellan Road, Newcastle. Tel: 01396–722599. Lunch on Sunday only in restaurant, bar lunches all week.

Culloden Hotel £££
Fresh local produce used in Mitre Restaurant – try Cream of Mitre soup.
Craigavad, Holywood. Tel: 01232–425223. Closed: Saturday lunchtime.

Daft Eddy's £
A trip across the causeway is worthwhile for steak, salmon, prawns.
Sketrick Island, Whiterock, Killinchy. Tel: 01238–541615. Closed: Sunday and Monday evenings.

Dickens £
General pub food to 9pm.
49 High Street, Holywood. Tel: 01232–428439.

Eastern Tandoori ££
Indian and European.
16 Castle Street, Newtownards. Tel: 01247–819541.

The Gaslamp £££
Baked trout in lime and walnut sauce, langoustines in cream and Chablis.
47 Court Street, Newtownards. Tel: 01247–811225. Closed: Sunday evening.

Granville Arms £
Hearty stews and à la carte.
Mary Street, Newry. Tel: 01693–61785.

Mario's £
Italian cuisine.
65 South Promenade, Newcastle. Tel: 01396–723912. Closed: Monday.

Old Schoolhouse £££
Interesting fresh food, traditionally cooked.
100 Ballydrain Road, Comber. Tel: 01238–541182. Closed: Monday.

Peppercorn ££
Serves unusual local produce in sauces made from dulse, an edible seaweed; also Guinness and oysters.
18 Kilmood Church Road, Killinchy. Tel: 01238–541472. Open: Wednesday to Saturday 7–10pm.

Portaferry Hotel ££
Stuffed mussels, oysters, turbot.
10 The Strand, Portaferry. Tel: 01247–728231.

The Red Pepper £££
Fish straight from the boats. Cheese fondue.
28 Main Street, Groomsport. Tel: 01247–270097. Closes: 10pm summer; reduced hours in winter.

CO FERMANAGH

Crow's Nest £
Extensive menu. Ulster breakfast all day.
12 High Street, Enniskillen. Tel: 01365–325252.

The Hollander ££
Specialities include beef Wellington and salmon en croûte.
5 Main Street, Irvinestown. Tel: 01365–621231. Closed: Sunday lunchtime.

Killyhevlin Hotel ££
Full à la carte menu. Moorings for visiting cruisers.
Dublin Road, Enniskillen. Tel: 01365–323481.

Manor House Hotel £££
Elegant dining on shores of Lough Erne.
Killadeas. Tel: 01365–621561.

Melvin House and Bar ££
Friendly hospitality and wholesome
home cooking.
*1 Townhall Street, Enniskillen. Tel:
01365–322040.*

CO LONDONDERRY
Beech Hill Country House £££
Adventurous menu; local produce
cooked nouvelle style; irresistible
desserts in fine 18th-century house in
13 hectares of woodland.
*32 Ardmore Road, Derry. Tel: 01504–
49279.*

Bells £££
Overlooks Lough Foyle and the city.
Local fish, rack of lamb.
*59 Victoria Road, Derry. Tel: 01504–
311500. Closed: Sunday lunchtime.*

Brown's ££
Rack of ribs, Caesar salad, vegetarian
dishes.
*1 Victoria Road, Derry. Tel: 01504–
45180. Closed: Monday.*

Cloisters £
Lasagne, macaroni bake.
*23 Church Street, Magherafelt. Tel:
01648–32257/33522.*

Fiolta's Bistro ££
Daily specials based on Co Londonderry
products augment full menu.
*4 Union Arcade, Magherafelt. Tel: 01648–
33522.*

Helen's ££
Chinese and European.
*440 Clooney Road, Ballykelly. Tel:
01504–762098.*

Macduff's £££
Local country produce, game in season
and Carrageen Moss, a traditional
Ulster dessert.
*Blackheath House, 112 Killeague Road,
Blackhill, Coleraine. Tel: 01265–68433.
No lunch served. Closed: Sunday and
Monday (except July and August).*

Metro Bar £
Try beef stew in Guinness.
*3–4 Bank Place, Londonderry. Tel:
01504–267401. Lunches only.*

Salmon Leap ££
Smoked fish, roast game in season.
*53 Castleroe Road, Coleraine. Tel: 01265–
52992.*

Waterfoot Hotel ££
Circular rooms on several levels
overlooking River Foyle. Local
vegetables, fish from the Foyle.
*Caw Roundabout, 14 Clooney Road,
Londonderry. Tel: 01504–45500.*

CO MONAGHAN
Andy's Restaurant ££
Six times Ulster Pub of the Year, also
National Hygiene Award winner.
*Market Square, Monaghan. Tel: 047–
82277. Closed: Monday evening.*

CO TYRONE
Le Curé Wine Bar £
Steaks, kebabs, vegetarian dishes.
*86 Chapel Street, Cookstown. Tel:
06487–62278.*

Greenvale Hotel ££
Homely atmosphere in former 19th-
century residence. Good à la carte
menu.
*57 Drum Road, Cookstown. Tel: 01648–
762243.*

Inn on the Park ££
Fine quality local produce used in
extensive à la carte menu.
*1 Moy Road, Dungannon. Tel: 01868–
725151.*

Mellon Country Inn £££
Opposite Ulster-American Folk Park.
Traditional food with French accent.
Non-meat dishes included in extensive
menu.
*134 Beltany Road, Omagh. Tel:
01662–661224.*

Hotels and Accommodation

*A*ccommodation standards, closely watched by tourism authorities in the Republic and Northern Ireland, are improving constantly, and there's a good range – everything from internationally rated de luxe hotels (though not so many of these as in other countries) to simple hostels.

Both Bord Fáilte and the Northern Ireland Tourist Board run registration schemes with official grading systems, and both publish lists of accommodation with details of facilities and maximum prices. Rates must be displayed in rooms.

The two organisations have jointly developed a computerised information and reservations system to which tourist information offices throughout Ireland are linked. Under the system – known as 'Gulliver' – visitors at the Giant's Causeway, for example, are able to book accommodation in Kinsale, Co Cork, or indeed anywhere else in Ireland. A small charge made at the time of booking is deducted from the subsequent account.

Reservations can also be made through Dublin Tourism's Central Reservations Service, Suffolk Street, Dublin 2 (tel: 01–605 7777) and at the Northern Ireland Tourist Board's information office, St Anne's Court, 59 North Street, Belfast, BT1 1NB (tel: 01232–246609).

The Republic also has Tel-A-Bed Ireland, an advance booking system for all types of accommodation (tel: 01–284 1765; open Monday to Friday 10am–1pm and 2–4pm).

Thomas Cook operate a hotel reservation desk at Dublin Airport.

HOTELS

Bord Fáilte has registered more than 650 hotels with a total of some 22,000 rooms. These range from the top-class international hotels found in Dublin and other cities and major towns, to simple provincial inns. Northern Ireland has well under 150 actual hotels listed, but this does not present much of a problem in a province which can be spanned in any direction in less than three hours by car.

The Republic has a good range of accommodation in country houses – often elegant old manor houses or historic castles – with excellent, even luxurious facilities. The houses are managed in many cases by the owners themselves, who go out of their way to create a house party atmosphere. Many places have indoor pools, gyms and exercise equipment, as well as excellent sporting facilities – hunting, shooting, fishing, golf – and offer high standards of cuisine.

The Hidden Ireland, Kensington Hall, Grove Park, Dublin 6 (tel: 01–668 6463) publishes a directory of 35 country houses. *The Blue Book*, published by the Irish Country Houses and Restaurants Association, Ardbraccan Glebe, Navan, Co Meath (tel: 046–23416) lists a similar number of properties.

The Shelbourne

Generally accepted as 'the most distinguished address in Ireland' and certainly one of the world's truly grand hotels, The Shelbourne, St Stephen's Green, Dublin, has been immortalised in literature, has witnessed dramatic moments in history and provided board and lodging for celebrities for almost 70 years.

William Makepeace Thackeray, George Moore and Oliver St John Gogarty all stayed at the hotel and wrote about it. Elizabeth Bowen was so enamoured of the place that she wrote a 200-page book about it, and James Joyce, who never actually stayed there, included it in *Two Gallants,* one of his *Dubliners* stories, and in his famous novel *Ulysses.*

During the Easter Rising of 1916 bullets rattled against the façade as rebels and British troops battled on St Stephen's Green. Guests were quietly moved to a room at the rear to continue afternoon tea. In 1922 the Constitution of the Irish Free State was drafted in

❖

THOMAS COOK
Traveller's Tip

Travellers who purchase their travel tickets from a Thomas Cook network location are entitled to use the services of any other Thomas Cook network location, free of charge, to make hotel reservations (see list on pages 188–9).

❖

the hotel. When civil war started, The Shelbourne was again in the thick of things.

The Shelbourne has been Dublin's premier hotel since 1824

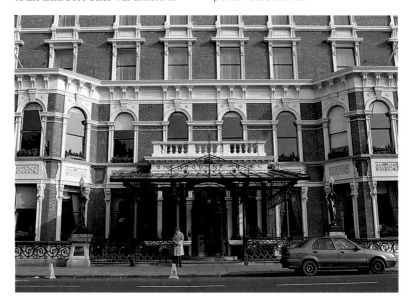

GUEST HOUSES

Guest houses are a less expensive alternative to hotels. The only difference in many cases will be in the provision of such facilities as reception areas, bars and public rooms. They consist of at least five bedrooms, often with en suite bathrooms, and guest facilities frequently include television and direct-dial telephones.

Typical town house hotel

BED AND BREAKFAST

This is probably the most popular accommodation option. B&Bs are abundant throughout the Republic, and increasing in Northern Ireland. In the Republic those approved by Bord Fáilte will display a shamrock logo.

B&Bs are officially categorised as town homes, country homes or farmhouses, but they may be no bigger than a rural bungalow with a spare bedroom. However, facilities in registered B&Bs will certainly be reasonable.

Many visitors to Ireland take pot luck with B&B accommodation, choosing a place at the end of each day's touring rather than booking ahead. But it is best not to leave it too late in the day.

FARMHOUSES

B&B apart, many farms now offer holiday accommodation on a stay-put basis. Evening meals – if the arrangement is not full board – are provided in many cases if notice is given before noon.

Peace and quiet in what may well be a very isolated location are obvious attractions, but for city dwellers at least there will be the added interest of experiencing life on the farm at first hand. Bord Fáilte is developing this concept of Green Tourism.

SELF-CATERING

Self-catering accommodation covers premises ranging from bungalows, old converted houses and semi-detached homes, to modern, purpose-designed properties built and maintained to high standards by consortia.

Members of the Irish Cottages and Holiday Homes Association each manage a minimum of eight purpose-built self-catering units. All are registered by Bord Fáilte and regional tourism organisations. Standards are high (though you might be expected to provide your own towels). Many properties built recently are attractive, comfortably furnished, well equipped and have plenty of parking space. Some new properties follow traditional styles of architecture, with thatched roofs, dormer windows and stable doors.

Restored traditional cottages in lovely

Ashton Grove Farmhouse, Knockraha, Co Cork, offers comfortable accommodation

rural locations, based on the French *gîtes* system, are available in Northern Ireland.

An option for those with grander self-catering ambitions is to rent a castle. Staff are available at some properties for those who cannot bear the thought of peeling their own potatoes or popping their own champagne corks (see Elegant Ireland address in box).

HOSTELS

An Oige, the Irish Youth Hostel Association, has 40 registered hostels, ranging from cottages and castles to former coastguard stations, schoolhouses, shooting lodges and military barracks. The hostels are available to members of the International Youth Hostels Federation (IYHF), and advance booking is advisable during the summer, especially at weekends.

Northern Ireland has nine hostels run by the Youth Hostels Association of Northern Ireland (YHANI). The Republic also has a large number of independent hostels. Many are members of the Association of Independent Hostels and provide good dormitory and private accommodation at budget prices (see Irish Budget Hostels address in box).

CAMPING

There are camping and caravan sites in 22 of the Republic's 26 counties, and in all six counties of Northern Ireland. The sites are officially regulated and inspected in the Republic and both tourist boards publish lists (see page 179).

INFORMATION

Farmhouses
Fáilte Tuathe (Irish Farm Holidays), Ashton Grove, Knockraha, Co Cork (tel: 021–821537).

Self-catering
Irish Cottage and Holiday Homes Association, Atlantic Apartotel Apartments, Bundoran, Co Donegal (tel: 072–41205).
Elegant Ireland, 15 Harcourt Street, Dublin 2 (tel: 01–475 1665).

Hostels
An Oige, 39 Mountjoy Square, Dublin 1 (tel: 01–830 4555).
YHANI, 56 Bradbury Place, Belfast BT7 1RU (tel: 01232–324733).
Irish Budget Hostels, Doolin Village, Co Clare (tel: 065–74006).

On Business

*U*ntil as recently as 20 years ago, Ireland's economy was based predominantly on agriculture. Since then, the Republic has diversified. International trading in manufactured goods, currency and commodities has contributed to a strong economy. A healthy trade surplus is equal to more than 11 per cent of the Gross National Product. The overall balance of payments is equivalent to 3 per cent of GNP.

The Irish have been full members of the European Community (now the European Union) since 1973, and as enthusiastic Europeans have been playing an active part in the development of the single market. As a nation, Ireland is committed to the policy of attracting new industries. It already hosts over 1,000 overseas companies, and more are showing an interest in the growing new International Services Centre under development at Dublin's Custom House Docks, as well as other locations in the Republic.

CONFERENCE FACILITIES

British companies and organisations have favoured Ireland as a conference destination for more than 30 years. Now business people from further afield are appreciating not only the facilities offered by top class hotels, but also the activities and sightseeing available near conference locations.

EDUCATION

Although the population is below four million, Ireland can boast the youngest population in Europe – half are under 28 years of age. It is also claimed they are the best educated in Europe.

Since 1980, 18 per cent of total government expenditure has been committed to education. A third university, Dublin City University, received its charter in 1989. In the same year, Trinity College's O'Reilly Institute for Communications and Technology was opened.

About 60,000 students are currently taking full-time, third-level courses, more than half of them in business, engineering, technology, computing and science disciplines.

Ireland has a higher graduate output per head of population than the United States. The ready availability of a well-educated young workforce is another factor which appeals to organisations considering Ireland as a base.

FLIGHTS

Dublin International Airport, 20 minutes from the city centre, has more than 100 flights a day. New York is a seven-hour flight away. Toronto, Chicago and Atlanta are within nine hours of Dublin. London is a 50-minute flight. Paris, Brussels and Amsterdam can be reached in 90 minutes. Geneva, Copenhagen, Frankfurt, Munich and Madrid are within 2 hours 30 minutes. It takes 2 hours 35 minutes to fly to Milan and 3 hours 10 minutes to Rome. There are 40 flights a day to London. (See also **First Steps – Arriving** page 18 and **Arriving** pages 178–9).

INDUSTRY

Responsible for attracting domestic and foreign manufacturing industries and financial service companies to establish themselves in Ireland, the Industrial Development Authority (IDA Ireland) has a key role in fostering and boosting the country's economy.

Backed by years of experience through 19 international and nine regional offices, IDA staff know the requirements of companies considering a base in Ireland. They respond to the need for quick decisions and a minimum of red tape.

The IDA's divisional structure – each division comprising a senior manager and a team of executives specialising in particular service and manufacturing industries – ensures that proposed projects are dealt with by the most appropriate section (see addresses in box).

ADDRESSES
IDA Ireland's head office is at Wilton Park House, Wilton Place, Dublin 2 (tel: 01–668 6633, fax: 01–660 3703). Overseas addresses:
Australia 38th Level, MLC Centre, Martin Place, Sydney, NSW 2000 (tel: 02–233 5999, fax: 02–221 8194)
Hong Kong 701 Ruttonjee House, 11 Duddell Street (tel: 845–1118, fax: 845–9240)
UK Ireland House, 150 New Bond Street, London W1Y 9FE (tel: 0171–629 5941, fax: 0171–629 4270).
US 2 Grand Central Towers, 140 East 45th Street, New York, NY 10017 (tel: 212/972 1000, fax: 212/687 8739)

MEDIA
See page 184.

TAX
Foreign companies are attracted to invest in Ireland by a variety of factors. One is a corporate tax rate of only 10 per cent – the lowest in the EU – to the year 2010, and the freedom to repatriate profits.

TELECOMMUNICATIONS
Investment of more than £2 billion during the 1980s has equipped Ireland with a sophisticated digital tele-communications system, making 90 per cent of the world's telephone subscribers, from Europe to the Far East, accessible through Ireland's International Direct Dialling system.

Computer-to-computer file transfer and video conferencing are available at tariffs claimed to be among the lowest in Europe.

The new International Financial Services Centre is connected nationally and internationally with a range of telex, digital data lines, packet switched data and voice private wires. (See also **Telephones** page 188.)

Dublin's Bank of Ireland

Practical Guide

ARRIVING
Documentation
British citizens born in the UK and travelling from Britain do not need a passport to enter the Republic or Northern Ireland, though it would be wise to carry some official form of identification – a driving licence, for example. Other EU visitors to Ireland must have a passport or suitable identity documents. Citizens from the US, Canada, Australia and New Zealand need a passport to enter either the Republic or Northern Ireland and can stay up to three months without a visa.

By air
Shannon International Airport is about 21km from Limerick. There are connecting flights to Dublin and other major centres. Taxis are located outside the main terminal building, and Bus Éireann Expressway has regular services to Limerick and other cities. The Limerick bus runs between 8am and midnight and the trip takes 40 minutes. The nearest railway station is Limerick, 2 hours 10 minutes from Dublin.

Dublin Airport is 10km from the city centre. Taxis are legion, but relatively expensive. Dublin Bus operates a half-hourly service to the city centre from 7.30am to 10.50pm daily. Journey time is about 30 minutes. There is an express bus (No 200) from Dublin to Belfast city centre (2 hours 45 minutes).

Horan International Airport, Knock, has a tourist information centre and car rental facilities, but not really convenient for those without a car. There are taxis and a local bus runs to Charlestown, 11km away. The nearest centre of any size is Sligo (51km north).

From Belfast International Airport, the regular Airbus shuttle service provides the best means of reaching Belfast, 30km away. The quickest way into Belfast from Belfast City Airport is by taxi.

Eglinton, Derry City's airport, is served by Loganair with flights from Manchester and Glasgow, and is a useful gateway to Donegal and the northwest. (See **First Steps – Arriving** page 18.)

MasterCard card holders and travellers purchasing their airline ticket from any Thomas Cook Network travel locations are not charged for re-routing or re-validation of tickets (see **Thomas Cook** pages 188–9).

By sea

Six ferry companies operate high-speed catamarans and jet-propelled craft as well as conventional vessels on eight routes between Britain and Ireland.

Using a conventional vessel, Irish Ferries takes about 3½ hours between Holyhead and Dublin. Stena Line operates high-speed and conventional craft between Holyhead and Dun Laoghaire with journey times from 99 minutes to 3½ hours. Both companies also run services to Rosslare – Irish Ferries from Pembroke, Stena Line from Fishguard – with similar crossing times.

Another operation from Wales is Swansea-Cork Ferries – 10 hours but saving a long drive for the southwest. Sailings mid-March to early January.

The quickest crossings are from Scotland. Stena Line and SeaCat Scotland operate between Stranraer and Belfast, taking 1½ or 3 hours. P&O Euopean Ferries sails between Cainryan and Larne in 2¼ hours.

Norse Irish Ferries takes 11 hours between Liverpool and Belfast.

Irish Ferries has summer sailings between Cork and Le Havre and Roscoff, and Brittany Ferries operates services from Cork to Roscoff and St Malo between March and October. (See **First Steps – Arriving** page 18.)

CAMPING AND CARAVANNING

Camping and caravan parks in the Republic are inspected and graded by Bord Fáilte and listed in its annual *Caravan and Camping Guide,* which covers 22 of the 26 counties. The guide is available at local tourist information offices. Some parks are open year round, but most only from May to September.

A central reservations service is offered by Irish Caravan Council Ltd/Caravan and Camping Holidays Ltd, 2 Offington Court, Sutton, Dublin 13 (tel: 01–832 3776). The organisation can arrange rental of mobile homes (on permanent sites), touring caravans and sited caravans, as well as the hiring of trailer tents, luxury camping kit and backpacking equipment. Other tent and equipment hirers are: Benbulben Caravans and Camping, Ballinode, Co Sligo, tel: 071–45618; O'Meara Holidays (I) Ltd, 26 Ossory Road, Dublin 3, tel: 01–836 3233 (branches in Cork and Limerick); and The Tent Shop (Cork) Ltd, Rutland Street, Cork City, tel: 021–965582.

The Northern Ireland Tourist Board lists about 125 camping and caravan parks in its guide, *Where to Stay in Northern Ireland,* some on sites owned by the provincial Forest Service. Visitors can stop overnight at most forest locations without a reservation, though this would obviously be inadvisable in high season. A visitor's casual permit covering a period from 2 to 14 nights guarantees a space. For details contact The Forest Service, Dundonald House (Room 34), Belfast BT4 3SB (tel: 01232–650111, ext 456).

CLIMATE

Ireland's weather is rarely extreme. The coldest months are January and February, when average temperatures range from

4°C to 7°C. In July and August, the warmest months, mean temperatures average between 14°C and 16°C. The driest area is the coastal strip near Dublin, where the average annual rainfall is less than 750mm. Rainfall in the west usually averages between 1,000mm and 1,300mm, exceeding 2,000mm in many mountainous districts. April is the driest month generally, with June the driest in many southern parts.

CONVERSION TABLES
See opposite.

CRIME
Visitors to Dublin are advised to be careful where they park and avoid leaving property visible in cars. Elsewhere, the Republic is one of the safest countries in Europe, though visitors should take the usual precautions against pickpockets or snatch-and-run thieves at large gatherings.

Petty crime against the individual is comparatively rare in Northern Ireland, although you can encounter pickpockets in busy shopping areas, and theft of cars or property from cars is on the increase.

CUSTOMS REGULATIONS
Both the Republic and Northern Ireland operate schemes under which travellers can claim a refund of Value Added Tax (VAT) on goods being taken abroad. Details are available at major stores.

TRAVELLERS WITH DISABILITIES
Facilities for visitors with disabilities are improving. Spaces are set aside in major car parks for vehicles carrying persons with disabilities, and an orange badge scheme allows drivers with disabilities on both sides of the border to park for

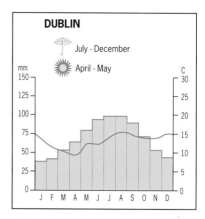

DUBLIN

July - December

April - May

WEATHER CONVERSION CHART
25.4mm = 1 inch
°F = 1.8 × °C + 32

free. Bord Fáilte provides an accommodation guide especially for people with disabilities, and a fact sheet. The National Rehabilitation Board, 24–5 Clyde Road, Ballsbridge, Dublin 2, publishes an access guide to Dublin and offers advice for visitors with disabilities. Wheelchairs may be hired from the Irish Wheelchair Association, Blackheath Drive, Clontarf, Dublin 3. Information and help is also available from the Northern Ireland Council on Disability, 2 Annadale Avenue, Belfast BT7 3RJ. Cars with hand controls can be rented from Avis Rent-A-Car, 1 Hanover Street, Dublin 2; or Hertz, 19 Hogan Place, Dublin 2.

DRIVING
Drive on the left on both sides of the border. Drivers and front-seat passengers must wear seat belts, and rear seat belts must be worn where fitted.

The Republic has three road

Conversion Table

FROM	TO	MULTIPLY BY
Inches	Centimetres	2.54
Feet	Metres	0.3048
Yards	Metres	0.9144
Miles	Kilometres	1.6090
Acres	Hectares	0.4047
Gallons	Litres	4.5460
Ounces	Grams	28.35
Pounds	Grams	453.6
Pounds	Kilograms	0.4536
Tons	Tonnes	1.0160

To convert back, for example from centimetres to inches, divide by the number in the third column.

Men's Suits

UK		36	38	40	42	44	46	48
Rest of Europe	46	48	50	52	54	56	58
US		36	38	40	42	44	46	48

Dress Sizes

UK		8	10	12	14	16	18
France		36	38	40	42	44	46
Italy		38	40	42	44	46	48
Rest of Europe		34	36	38	40	42	44
US		6	8	10	12	14	16

Men's Shirts

UK	14	14.5	15	15.5	16	16.5	17
Rest of Europe	36	37		38 39/40	41		42 43
US	14	14.5	15	15.5	16	16.5	17

Men's Shoes

UK		7	7.5 8.5		9.5	10.5	11
Rest of Europe	41	42	43		44		45 46
US		8	8.5 9.5		10.5	11.5	12

Women's Shoes

UK		4.5	5	5.5	6		6.5	7
Rest of Europe	38	38		39	39		40	41
US		6	6.5	7	7.5		8	8.5

CORK

September - January & March

April - May

BELMULLET

September - January

April - May

classifications: National Primary (shown with the prefix N and numbered 1 to 25), National Secondary (prefix N, numbered over 50), and Regional (prefix R).

Northern Ireland also has three road classifications: Motorways (prefix M) and A roads and B roads.

The AA has main offices at 23 Rock Hill, Blackrock, Dublin (tel: 01–283 3555); 12 Emmet Place, Cork (tel: 021–276922); and Fanum House, 108–10 Great Victoria Street, Belfast (tel: 01232–328924).

Breakdown

Drivers of rented cars should act according to the instructions included in their documentation. If you are driving your own vehicle and are a member of the AA or one of the AIT-affiliated driving clubs, you can call on the AA rescue service on both sides of the border.

Car hire

Major international rental consortia are represented throughout Ireland. A number of smaller local firms, who also operate under a code of conduct drawn up in the Republic by Bord Fáilte and the Car Rental Council, often offer cheaper deals, but may not let you do a one-way trip. Car hire is cheaper in Northern Ireland than in the Republic.

Documentation

You will need a valid driving licence and, if you are bringing your own vehicle, the registration document (or a letter of authority from the vehicle owner if it is not registered in your name), plus an insurance certificate valid for either the Republic or Northern Ireland.

Dublin's Ha'penny Bridge gets its name from the toll once levied on it

Fuel

Fuel is cheaper in Northern Ireland. There are now plenty of 24-hour stations on both sides of the border.

Insurance

Fully comprehensive cover is best, with collision damage waiver (CDW) if renting. Travel insurance does not usually cover travellers for third-party liability arising out of the use of a car; if you are hiring one, check that this is included in the hirer's insurance, or purchase a top-up policy before you travel. Check that insurance covers the Republic and Northern Ireland if you intend to cross the border.

Maximum speed limits

Republic (R), Northern Ireland (NI)
* 113kph dual carriageways and motorways (R, NI)
* 96kph country areas (NI)
* 48kph built up areas (R, NI)
* 64kph vehicles towing trailers (R)
* 88kph other roads unless otherwise indicated.

ELECTRICITY

Republic 220V AC (50 cycles).
Northern Ireland 240V AC.
Plugs everywhere are the UK standard style with three square pins; two-pin round sockets may still be found in some parts of the Republic.

EMBASSIES AND CONSULATES

Embassies in the Republic:

Australia Fitzwilliam House, Wilton Terrace, Dublin 2 (tel: 01–676 1517).
Canada 65 St Stephen's Green, Dublin 2 (tel: 01–478 1988).
UK Chancery, 31 Merrion Road, Dublin 4 (tel: 01–269 5211).

US 42 Elgin Road, Ballsbridge, Dublin 4 (tel: 01–668 8777).

Consular Offices for Northern Ireland:
Australian High Commission
Australia House, The Strand, London WC2B 4LA (tel: 0171–379 4334).
Canadian High Commission
Macdonald House, 1 Grosvenor Square, London W1X 0AB (tel: 0171–629 9492).
New Zealand High Commission
New Zealand House, Haymarket, London SW1Y 4TQ (tel: 0171–930 8422).
US Consulate
Queen's House, 14 Queen Street, Belfast BT1 6EQ (tel: 01232–328239).

Overseas embassies:
Australia and New Zealand 20 Arkana Street, Yarrulumla, Canberra 2600, ACT. Tel: 062–733 0222.
Canada 170 Metcalfe Street, Ottawa K2P 1P3, Ontario. Tel: 613/745 824.
UK 17 Grosvenor Place, London SW1X 7HR. Tel: 0171–235 2171.
US Embassy of Ireland, 2234 Massachussetts Avenue NW, Washington DC 20008. Tel: 202/462 3939 or 3942 (other consulates in Boston, Chicago, New York and San Francisco).

EMERGENCY TELEPHONE NUMBERS
Dial 999 for police, fire or ambulance services in both the Republic and Northern Ireland.

HEALTH AND INSURANCE
Under an EU reciprocal arrangement, visitors from EU countries are entitled to medical treatment in both the Republic and Northern Ireland, but should obtain a Form E111 from their own National Social Security Department or nearest post office before leaving home.

The form should be presented to the doctor if possible before treatment or a consultation starts. In the Republic you will need to make sure the doctor or dentist is registered with the Health Board Panel before seeking treatment under the reciprocal arrangement. In theory, UK visitors do not need to have a Form E111 – any form of identification is supposed to be acceptable.

Visitors from non-EU countries will need adequate medical insurance, and even EU citizens might be advised to seek additional cover. Medical insurance apart, a policy should include cover against third party liability, lost baggage and trip cancellation. If you do undergo treatment, make sure you keep all receipts to present with your insurance claim.

HITCH-HIKING
In the remoter parts of Ireland, hitching is the way the local people get around, but they have the advantage of being known to local drivers.

Strangers may not be so lucky, and might go a long time between lifts in places where the traffic is scant at the busiest of times. In Northern Ireland hitch-hikers may arouse suspicious feelings in both local people and the security forces.

LANGUAGE
English and Irish are both official languages in the Republic, and both are now taught in school. In the Gaeltacht areas of the west and north, Irish is likely to be the only language you will hear, and it may be the only one on the signposts. However, you will always find someone who speaks English. (See also page 185.)

LOST PROPERTY

Report serious losses – passport, credit cards, traveller's cheques – immediately. For lost passports, inform your embassy (see pages 182–3) which will be able to issue emergency documents. They may also be able to help with emergency funds if traveller's cheques are lost or stolen. (See also **Money Matters** below.)

MAPS AND GUIDES

Road maps of Ireland are freely available from car rental companies, but for larger scale regional and town maps the best sources would be the local tourist office, where there may be a charge. Book shops throughout Ireland usually have a good stock of commercially produced maps, including those published by the Ordnance Surveys in both Northern Ireland and the Republic. Guides covering the Ulster Way are published by the Sports Council for Northern Ireland, House of Sport, Upper Malone Road, Belfast BT9 5LA (tel: 01232–381222).

MEDIA

The Republic has four national morning newspapers: the *Irish Times, Irish Independent, Irish Press* and the *Cork Examiner.* There are two evening newspapers. Sunday newspapers include the *Sunday Tribune,* which carries good arts coverage, and the *Sunday Business Post,* which covers the arts and international affairs as well as financial matters. Provincial newspapers give a good insight into Irish life at grassroots level and reveal what is happening on the local entertainment scene.

The Republic has two television channels: RTE1 and RTE2. RTE stands for Radio Telefis Éireann, the state-owned broadcasting authority which had a monopoly of the radio network until the recent introduction of independent radio stations. UK radio and TV programmes can be received in most parts of Ireland.

In Northern Ireland the main daily newspaper is the middle-of-the-road evening *Belfast Telegraph.* The morning papers are the Republican *Irish News* and the Loyalist *News Letter.* Ulster TV is the regional commercial channel and the Province also receives programmes from the UK mainland and the Republic. The local BBC radio station is Radio Ulster and there are a number of independent stations.

MONEY MATTERS

The Irish pound, the punt, is divided into 100 pence, with coins of 1 penny, 2 pence, 5 pence, 10 pence, 20 pence, 50 pence and £1. The most frequently used notes are £5, £10 and £20. Sterling is the currency used in Northern Ireland and the coins and notes follow the same denominations as those in the Republic.

Banking hours in the Republic are 10am–12.30pm and 1.30–3.30pm weekdays, although most major branches do not close at lunchtime and remain open until 5pm on Thursdays. Sub-branches in villages will probably be open only on one or two days a week. In Northern Ireland the main branches are open 10am–3.30pm, Monday to Friday (up to 5pm on Thursdays).

Currency and traveller's cheques can be exchanged at foreign exchange desks at the international airports on both sides of the border. Before exchanging at a bank it may pay to compare rates. Currency can also be exchanged at some post offices and tourist information offices. Hotels will also exchange currency and traveller's cheques. Major credit cards are accepted throughout the island in hotels, large department stores and major restaurants. In Northern Ireland, MasterCard and Visa are the most readily accepted cards.

For loss or theft of MasterCard cards, tel: 1800–55–7378 (freephone). For loss or theft of Thomas Cook traveller's cheques in Northern Ireland, tel: 0800 622101 (freephone); in the Republic, tel: 00 44 1733 318950 (reverse charge). These are 24-hour services; report your loss within 24 hours.

The Thomas Cook Network travel locations (see pages 188–9) will provide emergency assistance in the event of loss or theft of MasterCard cards or Thomas Cook traveller's cheques, and to any travellers who have purchased their travel tickets from Thomas Cook.

NATIONAL HOLIDAYS
(NI) Northern Ireland only
(R) Republic only

New Year's Day 1 January
St Patrick's Day 17 March
Good Friday (R)
Easter Monday
May Day first Monday in May
Spring Bank Holiday (NI) last Monday in May
June Holiday (R) first Monday in June
Orangemen's Day (NI) 12 July
August Holiday (R) first Monday in August

Useful Words and Phrases	**Irish**	*pronunciation*	English
	Bord Fáilte	*bord fall-cha*	Irish Tourist Board
Like other people who are proud of their heritage, the Irish are pleased if visitors attempt a phrase or two, and a 'please' or 'thank you' in Irish goes a long way. Here are a few words you may come across (along with how they are pronounced):	**ceilidh**	*kaylee*	traditional dance or music evening
	Gaeilge	*gale-ghay*	the Irish language
	Gaeltacht	*gale-takht*	Irish-speaking area
	Garda Siochana	*gawdasheekawnah*	police
	fleadh	*flah*	traditional musical event or festival
	Taoiseac	*teeshock*	Prime Minister
	And here are a few you may care to try out:		
	tabhairne	*taw-er-nay*	pub
	slainte	*slawn-tay*	cheers
	mas e do thoil e	*maws eh duh hull eh*	please
	gura maith agat	*gurrah mah a-gut*	thank you
	la maith	*law mah*	good day
	slan	*slawn*	goodbye
	oiche mhaith	*ee-hay vah*	good night

Late Summer Holiday (NI) last
  Monday in August
October Holiday (R) last Monday in
  October
Christmas Day 25 December
St Stephen's Day (Boxing Day) 26
  December.

OPENING HOURS

Shops throughout Ireland are open
generally from 9am–5.30/6pm Monday
to Saturday, with some stores remaining
open until 8/9pm on Thursdays or
Fridays. Some places have early closing
on one day a week. In smaller towns and
rural areas in the Republic hours are
more flexible, and in many places the
general store will also be the local pub.
Pubs open in the Republic Monday to
Saturday 10.30am–11pm (11.30pm
summer time); Sunday 12.30–2pm and
4–11pm. Northern Ireland's pub hours
are 11.30am–11pm Monday to Saturday
with 30 minutes 'drinking-up' time.
Most pubs are open on Sundays 12.30–
2.30pm and 7–10pm.

ORGANISED TOURS

There is a wide range of organised tours
of Ireland, mostly by coach. About two
dozen companies are members of the
Irish Incoming Tour Operators'
Association, which works closely with
Bord Fáilte and the Northern Ireland
Tourist Board in maintaining standards
and promoting Ireland. For information
on guided tours in the Republic contact
CIE Tours International, 35 Lower
Abbey Street, Dublin (tel: 01–873 1100);
for Northern Ireland contact Ulsterbus
Travel Centre, Glengall Street, Belfast
(tel: 01232–320011 and 320574).

Cruising the Shannon can be an
unusual way to see Ireland. River barges
have been converted to give big boat

stability, luxurious accommodation and
haute cuisine meals.

Cruises are offered by three companies:
Shannon Barge Cruises, Ogannelloe,
Tuamgraney, Co Clare (tel: 0619–23044);
Shannon Barge Line, Main Street,
Carrick-on-Shannon, Co Leitrim (tel:
078–20520); and Shannon River Floatels,
Killaloe, Co Clare (tel: 061–376688).

The Dublin Heritage Trail bus calls
at 10 specially located stops, visiting the
main places of interest. There is a
continuous commentary, and passengers
can get on and off at their leisure.
Dublin Bus, 59 Upper O'Connell Street,
Dublin 1 (tel: 01–872 0000/873 4222).

Another interesting city tour is the
Dublin Literary Pub Crawl, in which
actors guide groups round hostelries
used by Beckett, Behan, Joyce and
others – and the characters they created
– and perform excerpts from their works
(tel: 01–454 0228).

Belfast has a narrated tour taking in
the city's history and its most recent
past, including the Shankhill and Falls
Roads. It is operated by Citybus Tours
(tel: 01232–458484).

PHARMACIES

Cosmetics, feminine hygiene products
and photographic film are stocked, as
well as prescription and non-
prescription drugs and medicines.
Contraceptives, now legal throughout
Ireland, may still be difficult to obtain in
parts of the Republic. When closed,
most pharmacies display a notice giving
the address of the nearest one open.

PLACES OF WORSHIP

Catholic and Protestant churches
abound, but there are few non-Christian
places of worship. Synagogues are to be
found in Belfast, Cork and Dublin.

POST OFFICES

The Republic's post offices are open 8am–5.30 or 6pm Monday to Saturday. Sub-post offices close at 1pm one day a week. The General Post Office in O'Connell Street, Dublin, is open 8am–8pm Monday to Saturday and 10.30am–6pm Sundays and public holidays.

In Northern Ireland post offices are open 9am–5.30pm Monday to Friday and 9am–1pm Saturday.

PUBLIC TRANSPORT

Air

Flights from Dublin to other airports in Ireland are operated by Aer Lingus and Ryanair. The Aran Islands are served daily from Galway by Aer Arann.

Bus

Bus Éireann (tel: 01–836 6111) operates a network of express routes serving most of the country. Dublin Bus (tel: 01–873 4222) serves the greater Dublin area. A four-day Dublin Explorer ticket covers travel on the suburban rail network as well as all Dublin buses. Ulsterbus (tel: 01232–320011) runs an express link between Belfast and 21 Northern Ireland towns. Unlimited travel tickets are available. (See **First Steps – Getting Around** page 19.)

Ferry services

Licensed boat services operate from the mainland to some islands, weather permitting. The main services are: Doolin-Inishmore and Inisheer (tel: 065–74455); Baltimore–Cape Clear (tel: 028–39119); Schull–Cape Clear (tel: 028–28138); Glengarriff–Garinish (tel: 027–63081); Burtonport–Arranmore (tel: 075–21532). Two important car ferries are between Ballyhack, Co Wexford and Passage East, Co Waterford (tel:

051–82480) and Killimer, Co Clare, and Tarbert, Co Kerry (tel: 065–53124). Crossing the Shannon estuary between Killimer and Tarbert saves 100km on the road journey.

Rail

Iarnród Éireann (tel: 01–836 6222) and Northern Ireland Railways (tel: 01232–230310) both offer special discounted rail tickets. The Irish Rover gives unlimited rail travel for 8 or 15 days throughout Ireland, and the Emerald Card covers island-wide bus and rail travel for similar periods. (See **First Steps – Getting Around** page 19.)

Taxis

Taxis are available in major towns, at taxi stands or outside hotels, as well as at airports, main railway stations and ports. Not all cabs have meters, so you may have to get some idea of the fare in advance. In Northern Ireland it is not unusual for customers to share the London-style black cabs.

SENIOR CITIZENS

Customers over 50 or 55 can obtain discounts from many car rental companies and from some hotels and tourist attractions. Several tour operators offer special spring and autumn packages for senior citizens.

STUDENT AND YOUTH TRAVEL

Members of An Oige (Irish Youth Hostels Association) or the Youth Hostels Association of Northern Ireland (for addresses see page 175) can get discounts on some ferry crossings, and holders of a valid International Student Identity Card can buy a Travelsave stamp which entitles them to savings of 50 per cent on Bus Éireann, Irish Rail

Dublin's DART system

tickets and Irish Ferries (between Britain and Ireland). Travelsave stamps can be purchased from USIT, 19 Ahton Quay, Dublin 2 (tel: 01–677 8117). Travel throughout Ireland is allowed with a Eurail Youthpass, available only to those who live outside Europe. The passes cover travel in 17 European countries and are available for varying periods. They can be purchased from travel agents, but must be bought before the traveller leaves home.

TELEPHONES
Public telephones from which internal and international calls can be made are abundant everywhere. Phonecards are obtainable from post offices, newsagents and other shops. Direct dialling is cheaper than going through an operator and private phones are cheaper to use than public ones. The cheapest rates are between 6pm and 8am weekdays, and the weekends. Hotels make hefty surcharges for calls made from rooms. Northern Ireland is part of the UK telephone system, so there are no special numbers for callers from the mainland to dial. Overseas callers to Ireland must first dial their international access code:
- **Australia** 0011
- **Canada and the US** 011

- **New Zealand** 00
- **UK** (Republic only) 00.

Then dial 353 for the Republic or 44 for Northern Ireland, followed by the full number minus the first zero of the area code. For international calls from Ireland, except to Britain, dial 00 in both Northern Ireland and the Republic, followed by the country code:
- **Australia** 61
- **Canada and the US** 1
- **New Zealand** 64.

Then dial the full number, omitting the first zero (does not apply to the US or Canada) of the area code.

To call the UK from the Republic dial 00 44, then the full number.

In the Republic dial 114 for the international operator and 1190 for directory inquiries, including Northern Ireland numbers. In Northern Ireland dial 100 for the operator, 192 for directory inquiries (including numbers in the Republic), 153 for international directory inquiries and 155 for the international operator.

THOMAS COOK
The following branches and Network partners of Thomas Cook will offer emergency assistance to MasterCard cardholders and travellers who have purchased their tickets from Thomas Cook. In addition, those locations in the Republic marked ★, and all locations in Northern Ireland, offer full foreign exchange facilities and will cash Thomas Cook traveller's cheques free of commission. Opening times are 9am–5.30pm, including Saturdays (branches of J Barter, 10am–1pm Saturdays).

Republic of Ireland
Thomas Cook, 118 Grafton Street, Dublin 2★; and 51 Grafton Street,

Dublin 2*.
Tommy Tobin Travel Ltd, 10 Chatham Lane, Dublin 2.
J Barter Travel Group, 92 Patrick Street, Cork*; Unit 2, Douglas Shopping Centre, Cork; 29 West Beach, Cobh, Co Cork.
Autoryan Travel, Unit 6a, Bandon Shopping Centre, Bandon, Co Cork.

Northern Ireland
Thomas Cook has both a foreign exchange bureau and a travel shop at Belfast International Airport. Other branches of Thomas Cook Travel can be found at: 11 Donegal Place, Belfast; 22–4 Lomard Street, Belfast; 39–41 Wellington Street, Ballymena; Unit 33, Bloomfield Shopping Centre, Bangor; 23 Kingsgate Street, Coleraine; 4 Bow Street, Lisburn; Unit 7, Quayside, Strand Road, Londonderry; and Unit 4, McGowan Buildings, Burroughs Place East, Portadown.

TIME
Both the Republic and Northern Ireland follow Greenwich Mean Time (GMT), but with clocks put forward one hour from late March to late October. Time difference with other countries are:
• **Australia** add 8 to 10 hours
• **Canada** subtract 3½ hours
• **New Zealand** add 12 hours
• **US** subtract 5 to 11 hours

TIPPING
Leave a tip of 10 to 15 per cent in hotels and restaurants, though some establishments include a service charge in the bill. Taxi drivers expect 10 per cent of the fare and hotel porters 50 pence a bag.

TOILETS
Public lavatories (in Irish *Fir* = Men, *Mná* = Women) will be clean and serviceable at tourist locations.

Otherwise, expect the worst and head for the nearest hotel or bar.

TOURIST OFFICES
Bord Fáilte and the Northern Ireland Tourist Board both maintain offices abroad. These can provide a wide range of information to help plan a visit.
Bord Fáilte
Australia 5th Level, 36 Carrington Street, Sydney, NSW 2000 (tel: 02– 299 6177).
Canada 160 Bloor Street, East Suite 1150, Toronto, Ontario M4W 1B9 (tel: 416/929 2777).
UK 150 New Bond Street, London W1Y 0AQ (tel: 0171–493 3201); 53 Castle Street, Belfast BT1 1GH (tel: 01232– 327888).
US 757 Third Avenue, New York, NY 10017 (tel: 212/418 0800).

Northern Ireland Tourist Board
Republic of Ireland 16 Nassau Street, Dublin 2 (tel: 01–679 1977).
UK 11 Berkeley Street, London W1X 5AD (tel: 0171–493 0601).
US 40 W 57th Street, 3rd Floor, New York, NY 10001 (tel: 212/686 6250).
There are about 100 tourist information offices throughout the Republic and another 30 or so in Northern Ireland. A third of them remain open throughout the year.
Bord Fáilte's main office is at Suffolk Street, Dublin 2 (tel: 01–602 4000). Northern Ireland Tourist Board's head office is at St Anne's Court, 59 North Street, Belfast BT1 1NB (tel: 01232–246609).
In London the All-Ireland Information Bureau, located at 12 Regent Street, London SW1Y 4PQ (tel: 0171–839 8416), handles inquiries about Ireland as a whole.

ACKNOWLEDGEMENTS
The Automobile Association wishes to thank the following organisations, libraries and photographers for their assistance in the preparation of this book.
AER LINGUS 18a; **BORD FAILTE** 32, 41, 42, 47, 60, 62, 63, 65a, 65b, 68a, 71b, 91, 138, 153, 175; **INTERNATIONAL PHOTOBANK**; **THE SLIDE FILE** 128; **WATERFORD CRYSTAL** 67.
The remaining photographs are held in the AA PHOTO LIBRARY with contributions from:
L BLAKE 50, 69a, 83, 157. J BLANDFORD 5, 16, 23, 67, 71a, 79, 104b, 123, 124, 125, 131, 155. D FORSS 39a, 48/9, 72, 76, 82. CHRIS HILL 1, 12, 17, 21, 28, 80, 84, 85, 87a, 87b, 88, 90, 93, 95, 98, 101, 102, 107, 110, 112, 113, 114, 115, 117, 129, 130, 136b, 139, 144, 145, 149, 150, 151, 152, 154a, 154b, 159, 160, 165, 167. STEFFAN HILL 11b, 18b, 19b, 20, 22a, 22b, 29c, 37b, 70, 73, 74, 75, 105a, 126, 127, 133b, 136a, 137b, 147a, 168, 185. J JENNINGS 2, 69b, 104a, 108a, 108b. G MUNDAY 10, 14, 15, 24, 26a, 26b, 28/9, 30, 33, 34, 38, 40, 45, 57, 100, 103, 104/5, 105b, 106, 109, 122, 147b. MICHAEL SHORT 4, 6, 13, 19a, 27, 29b, 35b, 36, 36/7, 37a, 37c, 39b, 44, 46, 48a, 51, 52, 53, 54, 55, 64, 66, 86, 137a, 142, 142/3, 143a, 143b, 146a, 146b, 173, 174, 177, 182, 188. W VOYSEY 9, 35a, 132, 133a. P ZOELLER 29a, 68b.

CONTRIBUTORS
Series adviser: Melissa Shales   **Copy editor**: Colin Follett   **Indexer**: Marie Lorimer
Thanks also to Eric and Ruth Bailey for their updating work on this revision